Families Matter,
YOU Matter!

Healing Relationships
One Heart at a Time

Christine Turner

D1157750

Copyright © 2020 by Christine Turner

All rights reserved. No part of this book may be used or reproduced in any manner whatsoever without written permission from Author Christine Turner, except as provided by the United State of America copyright law or in the case of brief quotations embodied in articles and reviews, with proper attribution.

The scanning, uploading and distribution of this book via the internet or any other means without the permission of the publisher is illegal and punishable by law.

Please purchase only authorized electronic editions and do not participate in or encourage electronic piracy of copyrighted materials. Your support of the author's rights is sincerely appreciated.

All scripture quotations, unless otherwise indicated, are taken from the Holy Bible, New International Version®, NIV®. Copyright ©1973, 1978, 1984, 2011 by Biblica, Inc.™ Used by permission of Zondervan. All rights reserved worldwide. www.zondervan.com The "NIV" and "New International Version" are trademarks registered in the United States Patent and Trademark Office by Biblica, Inc.™

Printed in the United States of America.

Due to the changing nature of online dynamics, websites, links, social media forums and references, no guarantee is made of the permanent reliability of these references.

All references are the opinion and personal experience of the author, Chris Turner.

Printed in the United States of America.
Manufactured in the United States of America.

Author Photo: Debbie McFarland, The Studio at Daisy Hill

ISBN: 978-1-7335754-1-6

Dedication

To Jeff, you are my love, my heart, and my joy.
Thank you for being my handsome husband.
To my students young and old…I hope I have demonstrated God's
love for each and every one of you. For those of you who want or
need more, this book is for you!

ACKNOWLEDGMENTS

I WILL BE FOREVER grateful to my friend Tammy Melton. Little did we know when we met as "newbie" teachers 30 years ago, that God had a long-term divine connection planned. Thank you for believing that God could and would use someone ordinary, like me, to teach others about his extraordinary love and power. Your generosity of offering your ministry space free of charge as a facility to hold my first, *Art From the Heart Workshop* changed the destiny of my and many other women's lives.

Thank you to all the fiercely brave women, who were willing to heal together in community during the first years of *Art from the Heart.* You will see that the pages within contain those things we learned together during our sacred time with one another.

Thank you to Debbie Gronner for providing me my very first opportunity to speak publicly and tell my story at *Women of the Well.*

To my family, I know you don't always "get" me, but you always support me, and I thank you! To my husband, I am your greatest fan and thank you for always being mine. This book could not have been written without you and especially the fine tooth editing and content support. I adore you my love.

To my writing coach Jacqueline Arnold. You helped me get unstuck and this book would not have been possible with you.

Thank you, Holy Spirit! I am sorry you had to shout at me two nights in a row for me to finally listen and write. I don't know what You will do with this, but I am glad I finally listened.

TABLE OF CONTENTS

INTRODUCTION

I FEEL COMPELLED TO write this book while in the midst of the COVID-19 epidemic. Having homeschooled my children, I know that too much togetherness can bring out dysfunction and conflict. Additionally, as we experience the effects of damage done to our economy, we may be "together" with our families more than ever. The effect of this togetherness will be difficult. You will need what is provided in this book; understanding of unhealthy behaviors, *why* we learned such behaviors in the first place, and how to heal our relationships in order to live in peace and harmony. Our situations may be challenging, and we may feel powerless to change some of our circumstances, but we do not have to endure the pain from dysfunction in our relationships. It is possible to improve and heal our family system dynamics.

The most powerful way to change your family, no matter your circumstances, is to work toward healing in *the absence of conflict*. This means we complete these lessons *before* we are in the drama and pain of hurtful words and negative emotions. If you are lucky to have healthy family dynamics, you too can follow these lessons to "fine-tune" those relationships.

Imagine how helpful it will be to understand toxic behaviors, why they are occurring, and actually know how to address them *BEFORE* everyone is upset. Families can use these lessons to initiate safe conversations on hard to discuss personal topics. When we teach our loved ones how we are going to deal with conflict *ahead of time*, we are planning to build healthy relationships. Children will need to be taught the basic concepts of these lessons, but they are not too young to learn what healthy interaction looks like.

As a teacher, I've partnered with over one-thousand families over the years. I was provided with deep insight into the hearts of children, and into the hearts of mothers and fathers. The stories that families tell display foundational fractures in our relationship dynamics. I've had a front row seat into toxic family dynamics, as well as the longing these families have to repair their broken relationships.

The connection I made with my students is a big reason I wrote this book. Simply put, my heart cries out to America's families and our damaged family systems. I wish I had words to tell you what it is like to listen to child after child cry in your arms. I could only grieve as I was helpless to do anything about it. Most of the time, the child couldn't do anything about it either. I felt that sharing my faith might help children handle their troubles, but that is not permitted in the public school system. All I could do is offer the children coping strategies on how to deal with events that should *NOT* be happening in the first place.

I've experienced the same heartache of my students from all viewpoints. I've been the shattered child, the comforting teacher, and the exhausted mom trying to create a "normal" family. My problem was that I had no idea what normal looked like. How could I? I grew up with sexual abuse, extreme dysfunction, and a volatile, angry father. Like many of us, because of my broken family relationships, I was crippled to some degree as I started my own family.

Good intentions are not enough to overcome the dynamics we carry from our family of origin. We have to examine our extended family dynamics and evaluate their effects on our family relationships today. These lessons will provide opportunities to shine the spotlight on these relationships. I believe that in doing so, we can change the way our families relate for the better.

I can testify it takes just one person to change negative family dynamics. When one person stops controlling and/or manipulating, it will affect the whole family system. We know this to be true. Just as one family member committing adultery or becoming an alcoholic affects the family negatively, so can one member choosing healthy change, transform the family in a positive way. Finally, by God's grace, I have good relationships with my family, and you can too!

In this book you will learn to identify unhealthy behaviors within families and to understand how those behaviors came to exist. You will learn what God says about families, healthy relational dynamics, and how to genuinely love your family. Above all, you will not just learn theory, but receive practical, applicable tools to develop healthy relational interactions.

The Beginning of it All

God began to teach *me* about love, control, and speaking honestly with my people. The scripture, "First take the plank out of your own eye before you tell your brother to take the speck out of his," (para. Matt. 7:3-4 NIV) applied to me. Or as my husband so eloquently put it… "Deal with your own s—t before you try to tell everyone how to deal with theirs." The reality is I cannot fix families nor can you. However, we can change ourselves and this will affect our relationships.

The start of this curriculum began with four women who met in my basement. They were my "Guinea pig" first support group. Little did I know that its success would bring more groups to follow. After writing my first book, *Beloved from the Start*, I wanted to develop something that could heal hearts from family dysfunction. The lessons that follow are a result of those meetings.

In our groups, we openly and honestly shared our deepest relational concerns. As it turned out, our biggest struggle wasn't about our past, but about present conflicts within our family. Our hearts were broken because our families were broken. We wanted to "DO" something to help, but we felt stuck. So, I asked God if He could help me create heart lessons that could heal families. This book was birthed…God inspired tools to reveal and heal family relationships and dynamics. The teacher in me knew that the best learning happens when we are able to deeply process information. Within the pages ahead are experiences to facilitate deep healing. They contain insight, stories about, and the whys of dysfunction.

This book is a hybrid. It is part story, part curriculum, and part experience. The goal is to equip the reader to make changes that heal. The lessons in this book are experiential. You will not just read the chapters but will also do a small art project or short writing assignment at the end of each chapter. The lessons are created to bring healing to families.

The lessons are designed to be completed individually, with a partner/friend/family member, as a Bible study, or in a small group setting. Small groups are crazy powerful for healing. Don't worry if you cannot imagine your family members joining you on this journey. If even one person in each family applies the concepts ahead, family relationships will improve.

Each lesson will focus on relational dynamics, respect for others, and communication. We will analyze the dynamics of healthy relationships vs. unhealthy relationships. We will compare our choices, words, and behaviors to what the Bible has to say about love and boundaries. Specific tools will be provided to enable change.

Art is a vital portion of this series because it connects us to the right side of our brain. This is the side that is creative, but also connects us to insight and intuition. Insight and intuition are some of the ways the Holy Spirit communicates with us. Even if you are not an artist; do not skip this vital heart connection. The art is process driven, not product driven. Most likely, nothing will be produced that will be "wall worthy." My hope is that the art will be "heart worthy" and forge a path to healthy family relationships.

At the end of each lesson, you will be instructed to ask God/The Holy Spirit to provide you with insight or direction. For some people this might seem strange. How can you "hear" the Holy Spirit? When one asks the Holy Spirit to show them something, you might have an image cross your mind, a memory of something might pop up, you may hear a word, phrase, or lyrics to a song. It will seem like it is just "you" thinking. Trust whatever you see, hear, or feel during these silent moments and include it in your art. It is connecting you to your insight and intuition. Sometimes you will draw a blank. When this happens, just go with what seems logical to you.

If you are a facilitator, bless you! You will find some tips at the back of the book. By reading the book in its entirety before beginning your sessions, you will become better acquainted with the resources available within the book, as well as those referenced elsewhere. If you have questions, reach out to me. For EVERYONE, there is a section at the end of the book just for you titled *YOU MATTER!* Treat it like a journal to document your thoughts, prayers, and most importantly the answers you receive from God!

So, be blessed, brave and get ready to have your heart's desire; a family that is able to sort through conflict and come out the other side still close and loving one another. Your family matters, and so do you!

CHAPTER 1

Family Systems Matter

Challenging Family Belief Systems

What to Expect:

IN THE CHAPTER AHEAD, we will first focus on what healthy families look like. Though it may seem like a pie in the sky ideal, that is our target for healing. We will then focus on unhealthy family dynamics, why they may exist, and how to heal them.

Objectives:

In this lesson we will explore the following:

- Families are designed as one of the ways God meets our needs here on Earth.
- Because of lack of trust in God, we interact with our families in unhealthy ways.
- What we think of as loving our family is not always love.
- We have fantasies which harm relationships regarding particular family members.
- We choose to control when we don't believe God is good and we don't believe He is powerful.

Loving Relationships

Just the basics of survival fill our daily lives. Working to provide shelter, food and clothing, consumes us and consumes most of our time. But our families deserve more than just the basics of survival. We can meet every physical need, even in abundance, yet be starving in our relationships. The connections we develop within our families' matter. Just think about it. Our behavior, words, decisions, and beliefs during the 18 years of child-raising will affect the future of our children and their children's children.

Our second priority in life, right behind God, is loving our families. We have a responsibility to those we love, to love and relate in healthy ways. We are meant to learn, love, reproduce, and eventually release our children to have their own lives. Families are our greatest blessings as well as the center of our deepest and longest felt emotional pains.

In every society, to the ends of the earth, the family is at the heart of each individual. Every culture agrees. Families matter, and the relationships between loved one's matter. Yet our families are floundering.

God designed our family systems. He created this community called "family" as a way to expand love. It is in families where we discover that love is not limited, but rather boundless. When we have a second child, we are often surprised that we love this child just as much as our first. Love is not something we portion until it runs out. When we give love away, we end up having more.

While God gave us families to love, He did not give us the ability to love them perfectly. He saves that distinction only for Himself. By design, we will all fail to love our families the way each individual desires or needs. If we were able to do so, then our loved ones would have no need for God; and God's highest good is to bring us to Himself. Our neediness is one of the tools God uses to drive us towards Him. Our intentions are good, but when we look around it is evident that good intentions are not enough to form healthy family systems.

One of our problems is that what we think of as love, is not always loving. Because I am writing this from a Christian point of view, every idea presented will try to look at our family systems through the lens of love. Why?

Because first and foremost, we love our families.

Of course we do! If love is key, and it is…let us have a truly clear definition of the term. What is love really? Is it love making your children and family members happy? If so, then we would serve our toddlers ice-cream for breakfast. Is love talking…and talking…and talking to your kids to convince them to change their behavior? Is love spanking your children with ever increasing severity if behavior does not change? Is love pretending that you don't see character flaws in your family members because you don't want to confront and hurt their feelings? After much thought, this is what I think the definition of love should be:

Love is speaking, behaving, and acting on behalf of another for their highest good.

"What the heck is highest good?" By this I mean the best long-term benefit for our family member.

In many situations we have choices that can bring about various levels of good. Often, these levels can equate to satisfying short-term happiness verses long-term growth.

Let's look at something simple like a baby sleeping through the night. The baby cries, mama comes, the baby is comforted. This is good. But there is another scenario. Baby cries, mama waits, baby self-soothes and falls back asleep. Which is the higher good, or in the long term the more beneficial? Is it more loving to train towards healthy sleep patterns, or to provide the short-term happiness in mother's arms?

What about going to the teacher on your child's behalf because of an unfair grade? A discussion happens and the grade is changed. A fair outcome is achieved…this is good. Or scenario two, your child goes in to speak to the teacher by himself in fear and trembling, and learns how to confront an authority figure in a respectful way. The grade is changed. Which is more loving? Which provides the greater long-term benefit or highest good?

Your college-aged child calls you with a huge problem. They have a week left until they get their monthly allowance, and they are "out of food." Choice one, send them the money, and they are fed. This is good. But what is the highest good? Is it not self-reliance and personal responsibility? And above that, is it not for them to know God as their provider? Is stepping in going to be *most* loving?

It is difficult for us to allow our college-aged child to go hungry. When our baby wakes up and we let him learn to cry it out, it breaks our heart. We want to intervene when our kids are being treated unfairly or are frightened. There isn't a "rule" that intervening in any of the above scenarios is "wrong" per se. What we look for is patterns over time. Patterns indicate a lack of learning which isn't in our loved one's best interest.

Healthy Families

The Role of Extended Family

The healthiest families have clearly defined roles within the immediate and extended family. We love one another and that is evident in our communication, behavior, and respect for boundaries. In relationships that function well, family members share common goals and work as a team.

Adults within our extended family do not make a habit of interfering with or controlling other adults. Love and faith are paramount, but faith is an action, not a theory. Rather than taking the role of preacher, i.e., the Junior Holy Spirit; we live our faith. Walking the walk, rather than talking the talk, is more important than trying to convince others to surrender to God.

When we are newly married, we are no longer controlled by our parents. Ideally, our extended family respects that though we may be young, we get to grow our family, figure out our relationships, and learn from our mistakes; just like our parents and grandparents before us. We may ask advice or seek wisdom from our parents, but unsolicited advice or interference should not be the norm.

Healthy Family Units

Within the immediate family, we have an order of priority with relationships. God is first. Then comes the husband/wife relationship because the most loving thing we can do for our children is to provide the stability of a strong marriage. Next in priority is the parent/child relationship. Parents love the child they have, not the child they imagine. The final priority, is loving, honoring, and serving extended family and those outside of the family. God is honored and our house is in order.

In healthy families, each member's contribution to the family is valued. Acceptance of each individual is paramount. We love our spouse for who they are, not what we want them to be. We allow children to grow in their God-given gifting rather than to try to form them into the kind of child we desire. We are learning what love is and is not and apply this to our families.

In healthy families our eyes can be opened to the ways we *ARE* being loved. When this happens, we become appreciative and grateful. Appreciation and gratitude are key components on how open your heart is to receiving love. For example, I thank [appreciation] my husband for his love actions...his doing the paperwork and bill paying, providing for our family, helping around the house, taking care of all the home repairs, protecting my sleep, or dropping everything to help me search for a misplaced item. Healthy families recognize when they are being loved [gratitude] and meditate on the loving gestures. Above all, healthy family members do not put the burden of "perfect" love on one another. "Perfect" love is reserved for our relationship with God.

Relationship Obstacles

Sometimes marriages have conflict even though our relational priorities are right. Why is this? Most of the time this is because reality doesn't jive with one's expected or "fantasy" regarding the marriage. Perceptions about day to day living, intimacy, and roles are fantasied about prior to marriage. The bar of expectation is set so to speak.

To compound the problem, during courtship we present our best selves. Boyfriends might bring flowers weekly. Girlfriends might "love" to watch football all weekend just to hang out. Over time though, we cannot maintain the same fervor, passion, and manners we did during the first year of dating. Boyfriends might happily sit for two hours while you try on dresses, husbands may not be so willing. The bar is set higher.

Over time, one realizes that their partner cannot meet or even get close to preconceived expectations. There is a reality adjustment we all must make in letting go of "the fantasy" and choosing to love "the reality" of the spouse we have. This is kind of a second marriage that happens in our heart. It is a pivotal point in successful marriages when we choose to "marry" the spouse we have, and cease trying to change them into an ideal.

For my husband and me, this pivotal point hit at the seven-year mark. I had a fantasy that Jeff would be the filler of my "love cup." I imagined us having deep, daily discussions and that he would satisfy my every need for love and intimacy. Because of my dysfunctional family background, I could not receive, nor did I understand the unconditional love God had for me. I was hungry for perfect love, approval, and unconditional acceptance. My poor husband was unable to meet these needs; only God can do this. I expected him to do so, anyway.

The "LOVE FIGHT" happened just about every month. I wouldn't "feel" loved, and I would criticize him and come up with a new hoop; if he would only jump through it, I would feel loved.

I prayed that God would help him to love me, and for one of the first times in my life, I heard an inner voice that I was sure was God. He said, "It is not him it is you. He accepts you as you are. You don't accept him as he is." With these words, I realized that my need was so great that no human could

*fill it. God enabled me to begin to let go of my "fantasy" and
accept the love I was being given in my marriage.*

Expecting Change

Sometimes we enter marriage with the idea that the person we have
chosen will change. When our spouse fails to change or to meet
our expectations/fantasies, we criticize and argue. There is a huge
amount of frustration because one honestly believes that if their
spouse would just do _____, all would be well.

Additionally, we can be blind to the varied and magnificent ways
we can love one another. We instinctively love our spouse the way
we want to be loved. Maybe we want affirmation and so we give
lots of compliments, or we value physical touch, so we cuddle, and
hug, hoping for our spouse to initiate affection in return. We often
demand love like dictators. "I feel loved by you exhibiting a certain
behavior (flowers, kisses, compliments, approval etc.) now give me
that behavior."

Life is good when our significant other demonstrates love toward
us in the way(s) we most desire. When that falls short, we also need
to recognize and meditate (appreciation and gratitude) on the ways
we *are* being loved.

For example, my husband's love language is acts of service. If we
had an argument, he would vacuum the house. Him vacuuming
for me was not my preferred love language, but he was still trying
to communicate his love for me. Through this act he was saying, "I
love you and I have heard you." Slowly, I began to stop insisting he
love me "MY" way and I began to appreciate the husband I have. I
have let go of my "fantasy deep communicator" husband. He loves
me, and listens to me, but I accept that he has an attention span for

about 10,000 words a day. That is why God gave me girlfriends for the other 20,000 words I need to express!

Parenting – Where's the Manual?

As children are added to the mix, new challenges are added as well. We bring to our marriages, ideas and beliefs about parenting. We have imagined what day to day life with children will look like. All of us could tell funny stories about our transition from the idyllic to the actual when it comes to having children; much like the funny, "What I expected/What I got," craze that is popular on social media.

This is a crucial time in marriages because there is a huge difference between the imagined and the actual workload of having children. Successful families navigate this by becoming a team, sharing the load. We learn to love sacrificially. Even though we may be exhausted, we step up to serve one another. Each parent reads and reacts to the other's energy level and frame of mind. When one parent has less to give, the other parent moves in and carries the load. Within the team there is an awareness and fairness where each parent takes the reins. There is no score keeping with, "We do things 50/50." Some days it is 70/30 or 10/90. The worst days are when we only have 40/40 to give and we need that extra 20% and we don't have it. When this happens, we need to go into hunker down mode. In hunker down mode our families need to rest, eat healthy, and cut off extra-curricular commitments until the family feels restored.

Parenting is the hardest job we will ever have with little training provided. What are our parenting styles? Have we given it much thought? Have we looked at how our own childhoods drive our parenting? Opposite day might be our goal now that we get our turn to parent…whatever my parents would have done in a given situation, I will now do the opposite. Nevertheless, our past motivates the ways we love in our homes.

Authoritarian vs. Permissive

What is your parenting style? Authoritarian or Permissive? What are the differences between the two? As a parent, are you more, "Spare the rod, spoil the child?" or "What can I do to make you happy my darling?" The New Testament speaks about not provoking your children to frustration. What does that even mean? Have you thought about it? How important is obeying? Communication? Is your focus on children following the rules to an expected outcome? Or is it on understanding and making sure your loved ones feel happy?

In the Old Testament, the law spoke of sparing the rod and spoiling the child. There is, and has been, much child abuse committed in the name of this scripture. Rather than its meaning, pay attention and provide appropriate consequences, it is taken literally. Sometimes, very angry people use this scripture as a basis to express their anger and displeasure in harmful ways.

Parents may want above all to have children who are respectful and Godly, however the only tool in the parental toolbox is punishment. Because communication is a one-way street, there is no relationship to develop other than that of parental authority over a submissive child. How children think and feel is of little concern. Spankings are given for every infraction, stink-eye, or door slam.

These children learn to obey, but fear their parents. Emotional pain and healthy communication go underground in this system. Respect is paramount and there is little give or take of communication. It is the parent's way or the highway.

The other parental extreme is permissiveness. Child-centric, the happiness of the littlest members of the home reign supreme. The child is the sun, and everyone is to revolve around his or her light. There is almost a panicky feeling when children fuss, cry, or are angry. The permissive parent searches to resolve the unhappiness.

For example, my daughter was a funny, funny toddler. She would count with me when I would give my warning count of three. She took the melted vanilla ice-cream out of the trash and spread it on her face and told me she was shaving. She drew a mustache on her brother's photograph when she was in the time-out chair. We thought she was hilarious, and it was difficult to discipline her. But right when she hit four years old, I had the realization that I wasn't doing her any favors. The rest of the world was not going to think her misbehavior was cute. My permissiveness was not love.

Permissive parents, like I tend to be, intervene in every situation and are angry when the world does not agree or honor the special status of their precious child. Selfishness and entitlement are the traits of children raised in this environment. They have come to believe the lie taught to them, that their own needs, wants, and desires are paramount.

There are two sides of the spectrum, authoritative and permissive. Most of us fall somewhere in the middle of these two extremes.

In the New Testament, the scripture tells us not to provoke, exasperate, or frustrate our children. This means that we are not to frustrate them so that they feel they cannot do anything right. Holding impossibly high standards, refusing to be flexible, not seeing and understanding the child you have, causes frustration in our kids that can drive them away from us, *as well as away from God.*

Tools for Healing

I am sure that at this point, there might be some relational dynamics that the Holy Spirit is wanting to heal or change. I know that this can be overwhelming and so I am providing tools to help heal your family systems. At the end of each lesson, I will feature a tool to heal. We will add in tools each week, but that does not mean that we neglect to use the tool learned in the prior week. A list of all the tools is explained in detail in the back of the book.

Tool # 1 - Giving Yourself Time

First, give yourself genuine gentleness and grace. We might feel like we have to fix-it, fix-it, fix-it. Hence, we take on the role the of fixer. The irony here, is that we are becoming aware of unhealthy dynamics in our homes and we want to fix it, yet we have no power to fix anyone. We would like to fix ourselves and we can't even do that. This is what leads to our broken hearts. Our healing comes in choosing new and better ways to respond to our families. Our greatest tool is Jesus and His abiding presence, giving us the power to respond differently than we have in the past.

So, give yourself *the gift of time.* We did not get where we are today in our unhealthy dynamics in a moment. We are in the process of healing and this process will draw us closer to God and closer to others. Give yourself genuine tenderness and grace. The process of healing from years of disfunction takes time.

♥ *Dear Jesus, thank you for showing me these things that need to be healed in my family. I present myself, my words, my heart, and my family to you. Please help me to be patient in this process. Inspire me when to speak and when to remain silent. Teach me how to act and when to let go. I can't fix anything, but I trust in your power.*

Tool # 2 - Giving up our Rights

There is something about saying these out loud to ourselves in the midst of persecution that allows us to continue to love and forgive. It prevents bitterness or thinking of ourselves as a victim. It enables us to speak truthfully because we choose to be honest for the other person's greater good even though there may be backlash. This is probably my favorite tool of all because of its power.

- We give up our right to be understood. Christ was not understood.
- We give up our right to be accepted. Christ was not accepted.
- We give up our right to be liked. Christ was not always liked.
- We give up our right to be validated. Christ was not validated.

There are two ways to utilize this. We can say it out loud amid mocking, rejection, scoffing, or name calling.

♥ *"Jesus, I give up my right to be understood. You were not understood, so why do think I have that right? I give up the right for _____ to "get" me. I give up the right to be accepted. You were not accepted by everyone and so I won't be either. I give up my right to be liked, not everyone liked you and not everyone will like me. I give up my right to be validated. You were not always validated, nor will I be."*

The other way to use this is to expect backlash when we make choices for our loved ones highest good. When people don't get their way, or they are called to account, or are confronted about their behavior, they will retaliate. They will twist our words or tell us that we are the problem. When our loved one slams the door, refuses to speak to us, or says they are not hungry and are punishing us by not eating dinner; we hold our ground. Just call out to yourself what it is.

- ♥ *"Oh, so this is the backlash this time." "Thank you for enabling me to give a consequence rather than stuffing my emotions and then raging later."*
- ♥ *"Thank you, God, and I give up my right to be like, loved, understood, accepted and validated. I make the choice to speak honestly with my loved ones. This is for their highest good. Thank you that you have given me the power and grace to be strong."*

Questions for Discussion

1. What do you think about the definition of love: *Love is speaking, behaving, and acting on behalf of another for their highest good?*

2. Do you agree that a "House in Order" is God first, husband and wife second, children third, and then others? How can you tell if the husband/wife relationship is a higher priority than the parent/children relationship?

3. Tell about the "fantasy" you had about what marriage would be like, or a "fantasy" you had regarding your child before you had him or her.

4. Do you remember a time when you felt that your parents "provoked you to frustration" or when you felt you would never make them happy regarding a particular situation?

5. Is there a "Junior Holy Spirit" in your family who uses scripture to try to control others? What does that look like?

6. Can you come up with a way for your family to determine and communicate their energy level like the 70/30, 10/90, and 40/40 example? How could that help your family?

ART CONNECTION

Permissive or Authoritarian?

Materials:

8.5 by 11-inch white or light-colored paper
Crayons, colored markers, colored pencils

Method: This art project is designed to illuminate what type of disciplinarian you are or what type of discipline your received as a child. The goal is to evaluate your parenting and discipline style in relationship to your family belief grid.

Where are you on the authoritative vs. permissive scale?

- Draw a series of thermometers, one to represent yourself, one to represent each of your parents, and one to represent your spouse (if applicable).
- Next label one side of each thermometer permissive parenting and the other side authoritative parenting.
- Pray silently and ask the Holy Spirit to show you where you fall in the range between permissive vs. authoritative parenting. Ask the Holy Spirit to show you where your parents were and where your husband might fall.
- When you have an image, ask the Holy Spirit if He wants to tell you why you fall in that spot.
- Then color in the thermometer.
- Wait silently until you feel led to begin.

Discuss and explain why you drew each particular thermometer. Ask questions.

Pray for one another at the end of the lesson as led by the Holy Spirit.

CHAPTER 2

The Process Matters

The Process of Christianity

What to Expect:

BECAUSE I AM BASING this book on a Biblical view, we have to examine our faith. If one has no faith, or follows or believes something other than Christianity, this chapter will explain Christianity and why Christians' actions sometimes do not match their beliefs.

Objectives:

In this lesson we will explore the following:

- Our actions, words, and choices are based on what we believe.
- In our family systems we have formed harmful beliefs that affect our relationships.
- Salvation is key and we understand there are two parts to Salvation, eternal salvation as well as the process of becoming Christ-like in our actions.
- We are assured of heaven and eternal life at salvation, but

our thoughts and beliefs are not "saved" or changed to be like Christ when we ask Him into our heart.

Salvation

We who follow Christ are in the process of our faith. This is a foundational concept in the New Testament, and it is often misunderstood. There are two parts of our faith. The first part is our instantaneous and miraculous new birth at salvation. Then, there is the messy and uncomfortable part, becoming like Jesus in our words and actions. As we live our day to day lives, we must confront our old self, trying to align our actions with Christ. It is uncomfortable, because the image of ourselves in the metaphorical mirror, resembles nothing like Jesus and we are disheartened. We know that He now lives in us and we have been given the power to be like Him, yet we fall so short.

When we first ask Jesus into our hearts and surrender our lives to Him, we receive a spiritual new birth.

> *God, has qualified you to share in the inheritance of his holy people in the kingdom of light. For He has rescued us from the dominion of darkness and brought us into the kingdom of the Son He loves, in whom we have redemption, the forgiveness of sins."*
> —Colossians 1:12-14

We are given something supernaturally at this moment, in fact, we are given many somethings in this moment. These somethings are a supernatural spiritual reality, like holiness, sanctification, power, and authority in Jesus's name. But they are mostly unseen in the physical.

Our relationship dynamics with God changes as well. Formerly, we were outsiders and not even able to see spiritual realities. We are now mysteriously considered to be both sons and children of God, with all the inheritance rights those positions assume; as well as having a husband/bride relationship, with all the intimacy that relationship entails.

These spiritual realities are *BIG…HUGE* and transcendent, and beyond any instantaneous grasp of our understanding. We are now in the process of our faith. The process of learning how God sees us and loves us is where we Christians are enabled to be more like Christ. This is where we go from broken to healed, rejected to accepted, and from powerless to powerful. God offers grace and so we are inclined to offer grace as well. We choose to offer Biblical love to others and learn to choose what is for our highest good.

In Hebrews, the Bible tells us that we are "perfect being made perfect." This means that we are "*in*" at salvation. We are *In* Christ and are going to heaven. God will never leave us nor forsake us. We are Holy, Perfect, Righteous, and Blameless. We are free from all judgement of past sin, as well as any heavenly penalty of future sin.

The world has trouble with Christians because the "being made perfect" part is messy. Oh, is it messy! All those imparted gifts from above have not yet been received in our hearts as true. Our spiritual reality has changed, but our belief systems and the ways we try to meet our own needs is not redeemed at Salvation.

Sin *ALWAYS* destroys. Living our lives with the damage done by our sinful choices, as well as the damage done when others sinned against us, is another messy part of the process. We may choose things that are bad for us, have false beliefs about God, and carry lies within our hearts because of our past family wounds. Heart wounds, the effects of rejection, abuse, and dysfunction can cause ugly choices and behavior. While there is no future heavenly penalty for sin after you are *IN* Christ, there are still the effects of sin…the negative consequences of sin.

God always allows us the free will of "choice." The beliefs within our heart drives our motivation, choices, and behaviors. When we live and make choices from our heart's unhealed lies, we are not Christ-like. Our behavior, words, and choices do not match the new "*US*" In Christ. We *ARE* hypocrites. Our actions, words and choices do not match the precepts of our faith. This is why our families are broken, because we bring our trauma and unhealed beliefs to our families and relationships.

The process of Salvation is often a struggle. At first, we might "try" to be like Jesus. Eventually, our "trying" will wear us out. We will come to a place where we ask Him to come and do it for us. This is the point where we learn to receive God's Grace, and ask for power, and love beyond our personal capabilities. We don't want to continue with the hypocrisy, but we have all this old baggage as well. We will still have times of brokenness when we are confronted with how lies from our past affects our choices. When we find our life floundering because of our independence or our insistence on meeting our own needs, we will need to change course.

Humanity *ALWAYS* lives out of what we believe. If we believe that Church attendance sanctifies us, we will be zealous to attend and judge those who do not. If we believe that every man will cheat on us, we may choose a cheater and then live a life of distrust in our marriage. If we believe deep within our heart that God is not good or powerful, we will live in constant control, exhausting ourselves trying to protect everyone and everything that we love.

So, there are two parts of the Christian walk. First, receiving Christ at Salvation…instant, imparted, holy perfection. Secondly, we are "being *made* perfect," the process of receiving healing and truth in exchange for lies within one's heart.

The Family Belief Grid

What we learned from our family of origin, is the greatest influencer of how we operate within our families today. Most of us believe that our parents tried their best. But this does not mean that we view our pasts with rose-colored glasses. We want honesty. Through honesty we can acknowledge areas that need improvement. We will look back and reflect on our family relationships and think about what we learned to believe about ourselves, our relationships, and God.

> *My belief grid belief used to be, "Only perfection is of true value." As a child, I was compared to others in whatever I did by my dad. Perfect grades were rewarded. My looks and weight were measured. My father was a fitness fanatic before there were fitness fanatics and no matter what I would do, the bar would be raised higher. If I ran three miles and shared my accomplishment, I was met with, "Tomorrow you can run four and if you carry a stopwatch you can better your time." It was exhausting, and yet I carried these beliefs into my home as an adult. Until this was revealed, I was unable to receive the unconditional love and acceptance of God. Neither was I able to give unconditional love nor acceptance to those I care about. I was not able to give what I did not have.*

The influence of our family of origin is so profound that many Christians still believe that the "sins of our fathers" are being visited on our current and subsequent generations. When we look at some of the ways our families function today, it might appear that those "past sins" are affecting our children even now. We see addictive behavior, explosive anger issues, promiscuity and divorce, children out of wed lock, and other negative traits present in generation after generation.

The good news is that sin patterns of the generations before us are *NOT* our inheritance if we are *IN* Christ and part of a new and better covenant.

> *"At that time," declares the Lord, "I will be the God of all the families of Israel, and they will be my people." ... "In those days people will no longer say, 'The parents have eaten sour grapes, and the children's teeth are set on edge." Instead, everyone will die for their own sin; whoever eats sour grapes, their own teeth will be set on edge... "The days are coming," declares the Lord, "when I will make a new covenant... "This is the covenant I will make with the people of Israel after that time," declares the Lord. "I will put my law in their minds and write it on their hearts. I will be their God, and they will be my people.*
> —Jerimiah 31:1 & 31:29-33, NIV

"Parents eating sour grapes and the children's teeth being set on edge," is a metaphor for children getting the consequences of the parent's sin under the Old Covenant. The passage goes on to say that "whoever eats sour grapes, their own teeth will be set on edge." Thus, in the New Covenant, whoever commits the sin will receive the consequences.

So, why are so many families functioning with the same negative traits and patterns as the generations before them? Our personalities, belief systems, likes and dislikes were formed in our homes. In fact, teachers know that by the age of five, personalities are developed within children. You can teach children, but you cannot change or have much impact on who they are.

Let's think about the ways our families solved conflict and how members communicated when they were upset, angry, or hurt. Many of us never learned how to appropriately express negative emotions, nor how to resolve issues as kids. Often, we apply the methods modeled in our family of origin, sometimes good, sometimes bad. Ideally, a family would be able to discuss problems, complaints, or "issues" openly, but this is not the situation in many of our homes. This is what has led to so many broken families and the deterioration of family relationships.

A grid system of belief is formed within families. A grid is like a sieve for spaghetti. Information filters through this grid, and ideas that don't align with your family belief grid are discarded. Thoughts, political affiliation, religious beliefs, and how we see ourselves, all filter through this grid of belief. Something might be true, but if that truth cannot pass through our family belief grid, it is nearly impossible to receive it in our heart unless we have God's intervention. I'll say it another way: *We can hear the truth, but it does not sink into our hearts.*

For me, I had foundational lies that lived in my heart. One of the those lies was "I make bad decisions." Like all children I blamed myself for the abuse that happened in my home. I did not have adult logic to understand what was going on, so I took on blame and responsibility. I decided that if I had not gotten into that bed when I was cold, then I wouldn't have been hurt. This lie, "I make bad decisions," went on to paralyze me. It effected my problem-solving ability and my ability to trust myself. Every decision caused tremendous anxiety and fear. The bigger the decision, the more afraid I felt. I was never able to make decisions until I dealt with this lie in my belief grid. It was not until I came to understand the how and why of this belief, that I was able to begin to trust my heart.

"What's in Your Wallet?" is a catchy ad for Capital One. "What's in Your Heart?" is my modification. Keep the following verses in mind as we discuss why it its critical to allow Truth to saturate our hearts.

> *Keep your heart with all diligence, For out of it spring the issues of life.*
> —Proverbs 4:23, NKJV

> *For the mouth speaks what the heart is full of.*
> —Luke 6:45, NIV

> *For as he thinketh in his heart, so is he.*
> —Proverbs 23:7, KJV

Many of us believe deep within our hearts the harshest words spoken over us. We all have labels from our childhoods, some seemed good, while others not so much so. Were you the: Smart one? Pretty one? Responsible one? The rebel? The rule-follower? The black sheep? The athlete? Labels from our families affect our hearts and core beliefs about ourselves and life. These labels, whether good or bad, affect the love and acceptance we have for ourselves, as well as the relationships with our families, with others, and with God.

Imagine, if in your family of origin, you were considered the dumb, black sheep. We compare that to what God says: you are a sought after, beloved child of God, who will never lack wisdom, if you rely on Him. Now comes the struggle. God's truth says that we are infinitely loved and infinitely valued; difficult to believe when our family grid tells us that we are the dumb, black sheep.

What if you believe that your value and family role is being the straight A student, and that you are the smart, responsible one? Because of the success implied by this label, it will be very difficult to believe that you have value apart from what you achieve. The unconditional love of God will be very difficult to receive when failure inevitably happens.

If we do not spend some time thinking about this, we will repeat negative cycles. If we choose to do nothing, we will operate by default mode, that is, we will act according to what was modeled to us in our family of origin.

The people closest to us are too important to just fly by the seat of our pants. Spending time thinking about what is good, loving, and healthy will reap rewards in the days ahead.

The Solution

The disconnect between our imparted identity given at Salvation, and our often-unloving behavior, changes over time with relationship and intimacy with God. As we know Jesus, we become like Him.

Beloved, now we are children of God; and it has not yet been revealed what we shall be, but we know that when He is revealed, we shall be like Him, for we shall see Him as He is.
—1 John 3:2, NKJV

All Christians are in the process of receiving and living as those loved by Christ. As we begin to live loved, wanted, and chosen by the Father, our belief grid changes. We learn to love. We learn to love God, love ourselves, and love others.

Review of Tools:

Review last week's tools: *Giving Yourself Time* and *Giving up Your Rights*. Were you able to use them? Were they helpful? Share if you were able to use any of the previously learned tools.

Tool # 3 - Talking to God /Prayer

Prayer is the weapon we have been given to fight the enemy. Entire books have been written on the subject. We have two lines of defense related to the concepts in this chapter. First, we learn what God says as truth and we compare it to what we are believing. We ask the Holy Spirit to teach us the truth. Second, we ask God which of our actions are based on lies from our past. We ask God to allow the truth to sink in our hearts. As the truth is received in the heart, we are changed in our actions.

This tool is the one most referred to by Christians, and yet the one we generally take for granted. Please referred to the appendix for more details and insight into prayer. Know this, if something matters to you, is troubling you, hurting you; it matters to God.

He is completely safe and wants to help you in every facet of your life. *PRAY!*

Tool # 4 - Saying What is "Most True"

Saying what is most true is very powerful. We use this technique as a part of prayer. While using it, we acknowledge the emotions and fear we may be feeling regarding a distressful situation and those feeling are true. We are feeling what we are feeling. But after we pray to God and tell Him the truth of our feelings, we then state to Him in prayer what is *MOST TRUE*. What is *MOST TRUE* is the truth of what God says in scripture. The promises of God, gifts of God, and spiritual and eternal realities are what are *MOST TRUE*. We then pray and declare the higher truth beyond our circumstances.

Rather than just claiming what God says is true, this process acknowledges the negative emotion that we feel during times of distress. When we say what is most true, we sit with the feelings and pain of a particular situation; but then we state God's truth which is a higher truth than what we feel.

♥ Sample Prayer: *"God it is true that my daughter is suffering from rejection and the effects of her childhood and being raised in our home. It is true that much of her pain is because of me and my brokenness and unhealed heart since I am her mother. But what is most true is that you are the redeemer of my life and her life. What is most true is that you are the God who saves to the utmost."*

Questions for Discussion

1. Can you think of something that seems good, but is a sin and destroys?

2. Can you talk about a time a trait of Jesus' was revealed to you by the Holy Spirit? Did it change you?

3. Think about and list all the imparted identity descriptors which happened instantly at Salvation. You may want to Google it and add to the list. For example:

   - You are perfect being made perfect. (Hebrews 10:14 NIV)
   - You are chosen, royal, a priest of God, Holy, God's special possession, in His light, and have mercy.
   - *But you are a chosen people, a royal priesthood, a holy nation, God's special possession, that you may declare the praises of Him who called you out of darkness into his wonderful light. Once you were not a people, but now you are the people of God; once you had not received mercy, but now you have received mercy. (1 Peter 9-10 NIV)*

4. Has God ever shown you something you were being hypocritical about? How did you discover it? How did it change you?

5. What was your role in your family? How does that affect your behavior and choices?

ART CONNECTION

Sorting God's Truth and Your Family Grid

Materials:

Pencil or Pen
Scissors
Small strips of paper 1 by 4-inch (white)
Styrofoam coffee cup
8.5 by 11-inch sheet of paper (red)

Method: As a group, brainstorm identity scriptures that we receive at Salvation. On a white board, or poster board, list all the identity changes. Feel free to refer to your Bible or use Google to expand your list. Complete the art project below.

- Draw and color, or cut out a heart.
- Then poke holes in the Styrofoam coffee cup to represent a colander that will symbolize your family belief grid.
- Write the "New Identity" phrases given from scripture on fortune cookie sized strips of paper.
- Then pray and ask the Holy Spirit to show you how each identity scripture is actually believed by you in your heart.
- Sort the identity scriptures into either the cup or the heart as follows.
- If you fully believe the identity then place the strip on the heart. If you partially believe it, place it next to heart.
  If you have not received the identity at all, place it in the cup. Do so with each identity strip.

Why did you sort the scriptures as you did? Did the Holy Spirit bring any word or image to your mind?

- Ask the Holy Spirit what in your belief grid is hindering you from receiving the truth of your new identity.
- Is there is a role you were assigned or lie you are believing? Is there something that is blocking you from receiving the truth? Are you able to replace it with what is true?

Pray for one another that your family grid would not limit you of receiving the truth in your heart about what God says about you.

CHAPTER 3

Boundaries Matter

Creating Healthy Relationship Boundaries

What to Expect:

BOUNDARIES MATTER IN FAMILIES because that is where we learn autonomy. Autonomy is having the ability to act according to one's personal values and in one's best interest. Autonomy also refers to having self-worth, self-control, and self-respect. Self-worth, self-control, and self-respect are vital to growing to full maturity and to full Christian maturity. In this chapter, some of the subtle ways that boundaries are broken are discussed. In Chapter Four, *Traits of Safe People*, we will look at specific behaviors that violate boundaries.

Objectives:

In this lesson we will explore the following:

- Healthy relationships include respect, trust, support, communication, and compromise.
- Struggling with boundaries leads to low self-esteem and problems in relationships.

- Gaslighting is a form of abuse.
- When we feel our boundaries violated, we can respond appropriately.
- Why control issues are a red flag.
- It is important to teach children boundaries and the consequences for crossing them.
- Using Spirituality or God's name to control others is spiritual abuse.

Traits of Good Relationships

Healthy boundaries are the foundation for the formation of healthy relationships. These relationships are ones where we feel loved, accepted, and even challenged to grow into our best selves. Yet, many of us struggle with forming these types of relationships.

We may long for close connections and intimacy with others, struggle to attain this, and become hopeless. In fact, hopelessness associated with being lonely is one of the leading causes of depression and suicide. Even though we can be surrounded by others, we may still feel lonely. Many of us feel this longing for connection, but fear the risk associated with allowing others to really know us.

On the other hand, some of us are social with everyone. We are willing to be vulnerable and tell how we really feel and what we really think, yet we are often betrayed. Our vulnerability is used by those we trust to hurt us. We need discernment. We need to be able to better decide who is safe. Who do we let in and who do we keep out in our relationships?

Trusting everyone with no discernment or staying isolated to keep away hurt, are *NOT* the answer to our needs. We need to understand and seek relationships which cause us to thrive. These will contain respect, trust, communication, support, and compromise. There needs to be mutual respect, even in adult/children relationships. Respect means we see value in another person, and we honor their wants and needs.

Unbreakable trust is essential for us to be vulnerable and close with others. In healthy relationships, we seek people who support us and want what is for our highest good. Rigidity will ruin our relationships, so compromise is necessary. And finally, we need significant others who are willing to communicate…even when it is uncomfortable.

Even if all these traits are present in our current relationships, we will still need to teach our loved ones our boundaries and limits.

Boundaries

There has been so much talk about "boundaries." The term was coined in 1992 by the best seller, *Boundaries: When to Say Yes, How to Say No to Take Control of Your Life* by Dr. Henry Cloud and Dr. John Townsend. In my opinion this book should be in every family library. The teachings from this book enables us to teach others how to respect boundaries.

So, what exactly are boundaries? Boundaries are limits of separation. They may be physical, social, or emotional. They delineate what belongs to us and what belongs to others. Respect for boundaries is key to the healthy formation of our psyche. When we struggle with self-worth and interpersonal relationships, it is often because our personal boundaries were not established nor respected as children. Without correction, we may raise our own children with blurry boundaries and a pattern of crossing them. Most of the time this is an unintended act. We are replicating the "normal" way of relating from our family systems. We do not realize we are crossing boundaries and do not see crossing boundaries as harmful or as sin.

Boundaries begin with our skin. Our skin is what contains "*US*" and separates us from another. Our skin contains our body, soul, and spirit. Our feelings live here, as do our thoughts. Biological processes like breathing, digesting, and feeling physical pain are within. Our personalities, likes and dislikes, humor, and even our quirks are formed within this place called our body. Our eternal spirit is centered here while on earth. It is the place where we love and nurture our relationship with God.

God gave us innate as well as learned abilities to instinctively protect ourselves. We blink, duck, and flinch automatically if it appears, we will be hit. When someone steps on our foot we say, "ouch" and we are *supposed* to say ouch. This may seem obvious… saying "ouch," and yet it is not necessarily the norm. Many of us believe that speaking up to tell others to stop something or to communicate displeasure is rude and offensive. It is like we allow others to be offensive, but we don't want to be offensive ourselves by speaking up about issues.

We teach people how to treat us. We use our voice to tell others when something is not okay. I remember telling a student who was mouthing off…

> *"My husband, doesn't speak to me like that, my kids don't speak to me like that, my dad doesn't speak to me like that, and YOU are NOT going to speak to me like that."*

Their eyes would grow wide, and they would nod their head as I taught them how to treat me. I had to have this "talk" at least once per year, and it never failed to change the way a disrespectful child spoke to me.

Some of our family members are perfectly charming and appropriate with others, while feeling free to cross boundaries with us. Why is this? It is because either the boundary hasn't been established, or it is being ignored. Simply put, they can get away with it.

The most immediate and clear way one's boundaries are crossed, is when one's skin is touched in a way that is unwelcome or violent. Physical and sexual abuse are the most obvious examples of such violation.

But what about when someone uses words to berate, manipulate, or coerce someone? What about when someone does not take what is clearly stated as a "No"? What happens when we push for our way even though we have heard the word "No"? Is this a violation of boundaries? Most of the time, the answer is yes.

It is vital to learn about boundaries because God wants us to have deep, safe relationships with others. Many of us struggle because we are not able to discern who is worthy of our trust. We either continually make bad choices regarding who to trust, or we keep everyone at arms-length because we cannot tell who is "safe" and who is not.

Gaslighting

One of the major reasons we lack discernment regarding who is safe and who isn't is because of something called gaslighting. Gaslighting is when someone causes another person to doubt their perception of reality. We become confused as children when the behavior of the adults in our lives does not match their words.

All abusers use this technique. They do something harmful,

but persuade the victim that what has occurred was caused by, or wanted by, the victim. We are not going to talk about the intentional use of gaslighting to harm others. Instead, we will discuss the "accidental" gaslighting that occurs in families.

Many of us have been told over and over again that our perception of what is occurring is incorrect. Sometimes, a parent who cannot handle the messiness of life inadvertently does this. This is the parent who does not allow the child to speak about their negative emotions. Parents may insist that their child be happy. They need their child to be "okay." When a parent believes that feelings are either good or bad, we have a problem.

Children might state the obvious or tell what they want or how they feel, but are told that, "No, they don't really want that," or, "No, they don't really feel that." They might even be told that what they observed with their own eyes didn't happen. For example:

> *A woman recalls asking her mom an important question when she was a girl. She wondered why her mom and dad hated one another. She was told that of course they didn't hate one another, they loved one another. She was gaslighted because the continual physical violence against her mother, as well as the cursing, name calling, and police intervention was sugar coated. It was covered over under the guise of we still "love" each other.*

When adult's words do not match their actions, or our emotions are corrected, the ability to trust is eroded. It is difficult to trust our gut, or intuition, or even the Holy Spirit, when we were told that our perceptions of reality are wrong.

Sometimes, there is a silent conspiracy to change the story in families. We were beaten, not because Dad is an angry drunk, but because we didn't have a clean enough room. When there is dysfunction and continual chaos within the home, the actual problem is not spoken or called out. Excuses are made for adults with anger issues, addictions, and those just emotionally cold and disconnected. Not only does this erode our ability to trust ourselves, but it also causes us to distrust others and even God.

How to Use our Words

Please, please, note, that honoring boundaries does not mean ending every flawed relationship. Every relationship has flaws in some way. We would be totally alone if we cast aside everyone who has ever hurt us. We understand that no one is perfectly trustworthy. Every person will disappoint us, hurt us, and at some point, break our trust. But we do need to learn to discern.

We can be really upset, and our loved one can have no idea. Most of the time, speaking up is the most appropriate and loving thing we do. We can have dialogue about how we interpreted particular words or actions. We can communicate what we need and listen to the perspective of the other side.

When we speak and clearly communicate our desires, wants, or needs and are blatantly ignored, our next action is to give a consequence. Like when you tell a child to do something and they ignore you. Or you have warned them about what will happen if they talk back again. Our words are not working, so we have to go to "Plan B." Taking away technology seems to have a dramatic effect in making children more respectful of boundaries.

This of course is more difficult with adults. We cannot *MAKE* anyone honor our boundaries. The only power we have in such situations is to put up with it, limit our relationship with the person to some degree, or withdraw from the relationship all together. Sometimes the boundary violation or toxicity in a family relationship needs to end immediately. This is a "911" type of situation. Physical abuse and the threat of violence, as well as sexual abuse, fall within this category. One needs to call the authorities and flee such situations.

Control Issues

Frequently, boundary issues are not physical in nature, but are the results of someone trying to manipulate another person. These fall under the category of emotional or psychological boundary violations. In these situations, we do not have to respond immediately. Often, we are not even aware of what we want or need. When someone tries to control us, it does not feel good, and yet it might be such a normal occurrence that one doesn't know why they are feeling this way. We might feel irritated, frustrated, or aggravated and not know why. We can allow time to think about our feelings and then set a boundary later when we figure out our discomfort and choose our response.

When we fail to address boundary issues, we may find ourselves suddenly blowing up at something small and insignificant. If you recognize this scenario, you are most likely a "stuffer." A stuffer is essentially one who internalizes emotions to the point that they eventually explode.

When negative emotions, like rage, wanting to scream the F-word, or wanting to slap someone happen suddenly; there is an ongoing crossing of our boundaries that we should have taken action about long ago. These feelings are the result of emotional buildup. This is a *HUGE* red flag; that we have been experiencing boundary issues that are ongoing and undealt with. We can use Tool # 5 - *Walking Back Negative Emotions,* to figure out who we need to speak with and why. If children are involved, it is time to give a consequence.

Stuffers, like I was, believe that they can talk someone out of bad behavior. We avoid conflict and don't want unhappiness or backlash. When we follow through on our threats and give our loved ones' consequences; they pout, complain, argue, and whine. So instead; we stuff, lecture, sermonize, and have long heart to heart talks. We believe if we can just get an individual to "understand," we can then get the person to change his or her behavior.

Probably the worst thing that happens when we stuff and then blowup, is that we also "blowup" our leg to stand on.

> *I would tell my children to pick-up after themselves. The next day, I would point out their unmade beds and pigsty floor, then talk about how nice it is to go to sleep in a nicely made bed with a tidy room. The day after that, I would remind them of how hard I work to keep a nice home for them and that they better get it clean by tomorrow. On Saturday, I would ask if they had cleaned their room and they would say yes. I would go up to check, and their room was still a disaster. Then I would go crazy! I would begin screaming… "Get up here and get this F—ing room cleaned this instant. This room is a blankety blank mess. I told you to clean it how many times?"*
>
> *They would come up and say something like, "Gosh mom, Chill. Nice language. And you call yourself a Christian." I would end up apologizing for cursing!*

My stuffing and the resulting explosion, thus, blew up my leg to stand on. Rather than the problem being about ignoring and disrespecting my boundaries, it became about my inappropriate anger and foul language. If I had just given a consequence as soon as my directions were disregarded, all our mutual boundary issues would have been avoided.

As I learned to deal with stuffing, I paid close attention to when I was about to explode. When I felt that rage bubbling up and the sensation of trying to reason with myself and not speak, I knew it was time to take an action. I would take a few moments and think about what repeated boundary violation had occurred over the last few days. Was it being ignored? A reoccurring tone of disrespect and back talk? Constant bickering between the kids? A bad attitude? Once I had insight, I wouldn't give an immediate lecture or consequence. Instead, I would wait and be ready. I couldn't go back and punish for what I had let go in the days prior. It would be like spanking a dog after the fact. No, I would be ready and know what boundary issue was causing the feelings to build up. The second the issue reoccurred…consequence time.

There would be shock from my kids that they were getting a consequence so quickly. They were puzzled, because I was changing the rules. In the past they had learned that I only "meant it" when I was beside myself with rage. Now, they were having to learn to honor my words and boundaries.

Self-awareness and preparation are incredibly powerful. It completely relieves the feeling of resentment and rage that stuffing brings. Try it! Crazy powerful.

This process of taking time and figuring out why we feel so angry and frustrated is not just for use with children. Often, there are people in our adult circles, or work settings that take advantage of, or disrespect us. Taking time to figure out where our boundaries are being crossed and being prepared for the future is helpful. It heals the boundary violation pattern others have with us. It also stops us from being the violators when we stuff and then blowup at others.

If we are not in an emergency, physical safety type of boundary crossing situation, we always have time. We can analyze and determine what action to take. We decide if we care enough to confront an issue. If we have no real or deep relationship, we may choose to let something go because the relationship is not meaningful enough to warrant confrontation. During our assessment, we can consider how we feel. It is okay to tell someone we need a few moments or ask if we can get back with them before we speak.

People who cross boundaries are sometimes trying to control a situation. It may be that they just want their own way. They may believe that they are "right" regarding what should happen in a particular situation. Controlling and trying to control others is a red flag because it doesn't come from God. Remember, God does not control us. We are completely free to choose our words and actions. We are also free to choose the big things in life, like our beliefs and our faith.

Children and Boundaries

There are times when we control others. It is appropriate to make choices for children who do not have the ability to choose what is best for them. Children build trust and feel safe when clear boundaries are established and when the adults in their life are clear about right and wrong. Kids feel safe when the adults in their lives are confident leaders, respectful in their communication, and give appropriate consequences for misbehavior.

Children will test limits set by adults to learn the rules of engagement and the consequences of disobedience. Ask any teacher what it is like at the beginning of the year. The entire class wants to *KNOW* the expectations of the new teacher. Good teachers spend the first week setting boundaries, teaching rules, and the resultant consequences for misbehavior.

Then comes the testing of those boundaries! Watching closely as peers interact with one another, each child is taking careful note as to what happens when students test the limits. Does the teacher follow through? Does she scream? Does she shame the child in front of the class as a means of control? Does she hold a grudge? Are the consequences given fairly and evenly distributed, or are there favorites to whom the rules do not apply? All are deciding if the environment and their teacher are "safe."

Spiritual Boundaries

As it goes in the classroom, so it is in the home. The family learns boundaries or the lack thereof, and either thrives or flounders in their relationships.

Like many, I came from a home where there was little understanding of boundaries. Several types of abuse were present, and I knew no other way to interact than what I had learned within my family. Slowly, I began to take steps to become a person who truly respected others.

> *As awareness dawned and I learned about boundaries, I began to apologize to my family for trying to control everyone. The ironic thing was that I was so good at it. I would use compliments and praise to try to get everybody*

*to do my will. I honestly thought that "my will" was right.
Probably the way that I crossed boundaries the most was
through Spiritual Abuse.*

Spiritual Abuse is a subject all on its own. In short, it manifests
when one believes they are spiritually superior to another. When one
believes that they are higher than another person spirituality, they
often use God or His word to control or manipulate others.

We all grow in maturity, wisdom, and understanding within our
Christian beliefs. The Bible says that all of us who are Christian are "In
Christ." If you are "in" something, you are enclosed…completely surrounded. One is not more enclosed than another if they are enclosed.
I think of the faith walk as comparing two oak trees, a baby oak tree,
and a full-grown oak tree. Which is the superior oak tree? They are
equal, both perfect oaks. That is their DNA…oak trees. Our DNA as
Christians is "IN Christ." One might be more mature or seek deeper
intimacy, but no Christian is superior to another believer.

The trump card of all trump cards in spiritual abuse is played
when someone says, "God says…" or "God wants you to…" or "God
told me to tell you…" This closes all dialogue and effectively shuts
down free-will, because if "God said…" then there is no argument.
He is the highest of the high.

Prior to my awakening, I felt responsible for the Spiritual formation
of my kids. I took seriously my responsibility to teach my children
the way they should go. But I ended up using God and His word
to criticize my family. We are supposed to *model* our faith to our
children. This modeling can become twisted when we try to do God's
job. We often feel responsible for our children's faith and heart beliefs.
The faith and heart of our loved one's is God's responsibility not ours.

Many Christian mothers, like I am, have good intentions.

Unfortunately, we step out of our lane and become the Junior Holy Spirit to our family. This is a huge boundary issue. We tack on little bits of Bible verse and inadvertently sow condemnation as we go about mothering.

> *Healthy changes for me required humbling myself. As I got better, the entire family system got healthier. I began to model Jesus and allow others to truly have free will. When I would catch myself manipulating, giving unsolicited advice, or preaching at my children, I would apologize. As I learned to tell the kids why my past behavior was wrong, we began to build a trusting, mutual relationship. Through this, my children learned how to respect others in new ways. Basically, as I became healthier, the whole family became healthier. I was on the way to becoming a safe person.*
>
> *My resigning from the role of Junior Holy Spirit actually allowed them to decide if they were going to choose God or not. There was a resentment and tainting of who God really is, because I used Him to critique and control my family.*

This humbling oneself is the path to restoration. It is the change in us that changes our family dynamic and heals our families. It is especially powerful with teens and young adults. As we learn to become safe people (like in the chapter ahead) and honestly, humbly, and verbally own our boundary violations, healing begins. When God heals us to the point that we can explain our personal journey to wholeness, there is a transparency and vulnerability that softens hardened hearts. We are knocked off our self-imposed pedestal and allow our kids to discover that we are also on our own sometimes flawed faith-walk, just like them.

Review of Tools:

Review last week's tools: *Talking to God/Prayer* and *Saying What is "Most True."* Were you able to use them? Were they helpful? Share if you were able to use any of previously learned tools.

Tool # 5 - Walking Back Negative Emotions

Negative emotions are trying to tell us something. Feelings follow thoughts. Think about this because it is really important. Feelings follow thoughts. If you feel sad, angry, frustrated, or helpless, did it not first originate in your mind? Did you not first ruminate on something that scared you, or that you want to fix, or something about which you feel shame? Can you feel angry if you have not first had an angry thought? No, it all originates in the mind.

We often try to override our negative feelings to rush to feel good. We use stuffing, denial, avoid our legitimate feelings of depression and anger, or just use our most favorite distraction, to avoid dealing with pain and discomfort. By investigating our feelings, we can decide three things. Do we need to confront something? Do we need to allow ourselves to feel sad, or angry over an issue? Or do we need to reframe negative thoughts into positive ones?

This is the process. Once we know why we feel what we are feeling, we can then rationally choose how to respond or act with our family.

- I feel _____ right now. (Negative emotion). Why do I feel _____?
- What have I been thinking about?
- When did this feeling start?

- What occurred right before the feeling?
- What is the belief or thought behind the feeling?

Ponder the answers to the above questions. Then ask:

- Is this related to my family belief system?
- What am I afraid of?
- What are my choices in this situation?
- What is God's highest good?
- Is what I am believing true?

Tool # 6 - Holding up a Hand

Holding up a hand is a physical technique used to create a boundary between you and another person. Boundary resistant individuals are often unaware of their behavior. Using this technique provides a non-verbal cue to the boundary resistant, that they need to stop or change their behavior.

This is a very effective technique when someone refuses to take your "no," or disrespects what you are saying. It is to be used with words spoken by you in a commanding voice. It places a physical boundary and puts the other person at arms-length. Thus, it emphasizes that you mean what you say, and that the other person is crossing your boundary.

- To use it, stretch out your arm full length and turn your hand at a 90-degree angle so fingers point upward. Fingers will be splayed in the classic "Stop Sign" position.
- Place your hand so that it breaks eye contact with the individual you are confronting.

- Firmly state what the person is doing wrong:
  - "I said, "NO.""
  - "Don't ask me again."
  - "Do not speak to me in that tone."
  - "I am going to leave until you can speak to me without yelling."

Questions for Discussion

1. Why is respect, trust, support, communication, and compromise paramount if boundaries are to be respected?

2. Who in your family relationships is most likely to fail to communicate what they want and need?

3. Why do so many people not take a "No" or try to talk someone out of their "No?" What do you think is underneath this spiritually?

4. Do you know someone who is perfectly charming with most people, but they are disrespectful to you? To somebody else?

5. Can you share a time when you were gaslighted? How did that affect you?

6. Are you a stuffer? What are the physical and emotional signs that indicate you might blowup?

7. Have you ever been spiritually abused? How did that affect your relationship with other Christians? With God?

ART CONNECTION

"Talk to the Hand"

Materials:

Markers, crayons, colored paper
8.5 by 11-inch sheet of paper (white)

Method: This project will give you the opportunity to evaluate who in your life is disrespecting boundaries.

- Trace your hand on a piece of 8.5 by 11-inch sheet of paper. In the center of the hand write the word "No."
- Pray and ask the Holy Spirit to show you who you need to hold this symbolic "hand" up to in your life. What do you need to say? When do you need to say it?
- When you feel that you have an image in your mind, write down on each finger who or what situations you feel need better boundaries.

If doing this in a small group, share your creations and insight. Listen and ask questions. Pray for one another.

CHAPTER 4

Safety Matters

Traits of Safe People

What to Expect:

WE ALL WANT TO be trustworthy people. Sometimes we begin a relationship full of trust only to discover that the trust has eroded over time. This is because the person in your relationship is demonstrating some of the unsafe behaviors listed in the pages to follow. In this chapter, you will identify many acquaintances and family members who have unsafe traits. Remember though, this lesson is not for "everyone else." We can only change ourselves. We first deal with our own "s—t" before we tell others to deal with theirs. We want to be models of safe, reliable, healthy, and trustworthy behavior.

Objectives:

In this lesson we will explore the following:

- "Safe" people have traits that demonstrate trustworthiness.
- Jesus had boundaries.
- When our boundaries were crossed as children, it makes it difficult to discern who to trust.

- We may need to change to become "safe."

Safe: a safe place; free from hurt, harm, injury, danger, or risk: https://www.dictionary.com

Safety, It Starts with Us

Seeking change and God dealing with my hypocrisy is where my journey began. Fifteen years ago, I read Dr. Henry Cloud and Dr. John Townsend's books *Boundaries* and *Safe People*. I am forever grateful to them because their work started true healing within me. I wasn't a safe person. God confronted me on how I was treating others; my behavior, my gossip and my oh so often unwanted and unsolicited advice. I was able to make some necessary changes. It has been a good, yet sobering journey and through it, I got my family back!

Levels of Safe

Jesus modeled the intimacy of relationships and demonstrated that there are levels to safe people. He was closest to The Father, the safest one. He then had three disciples: Peter, James, and John. This was His inner circle, those who He trusted most. Next, He had the twelve apostles, including Judas, who was untrustworthy and though he betrayed Jesus, was pivotal in bringing about Jesus's destiny. (We all have our Judases don't we? People who break our trust, sin against us, and yet drive us into the arms of God.) After the twelve, were the 70 disciples who went out in Jesus' name. Finally, there were the multitudes; the masses that showed up for food, followed Jesus around, or ignored Him altogether.

Traits of Safe People

The descriptors ahead may hit you hard. They did me. I don't speak on this as one who has it all together. Learning about these traits humbled me and caused me to change. I am still learning to become a safer person. The following pages are traits of safe people. This list is to be used two ways.

- God might inspire you to seek to change and heal. You might discover you need to become and model "safe" within your family system.
- This list can be used to detach and discern how close we should let others get to our hearts. Not everyone should be in the inner circle of our lives.

Safe People respect what another person says, especially when it comes to how they feel. One might ask questions to understand and validate how someone feels, but they don't say, "You don't feel this," or "You shouldn't feel that." There is no need put a value statement on feelings. Feelings are feelings and will ebb and flow. We all have bad days or blue moments. Often, a negative feeling is the entirely appropriate emotion for what you've experienced. Failure to allow others to appropriately process negative emotions can cause them to get stuck and not heal from emotional wounds.

Safe People follow through on their word and their commitments. Many times, we fail to follow through on what we said we were going to do. This can be because we are overly optimistic or are poor planners and overschedule ourselves. Sometimes we say yes because we feel like people will feel disappointed if we say no. After the fact, we come up with an excuse and fail to show up or fulfill our word. We are not always able to perfectly fulfill our word. When we fail to do so, we recognize our failure and own it. We verbally apologize and acknowledge our failings.

Safe People allow others to "not be okay." Sometimes, it frightens us when someone we love is suffering. Let's face it, when a loved one suffers, we suffer…and *WE DON'T LIKE SUFFERING.* There are rough patches in life when we are not okay, and we need to allow ourselves and others to not be okay. We don't stay there, and we don't let loved ones stay there, but we allow some time for loved ones to process negative emotions.

> *An example of this is when my husband and I would argue. I wanted to rush to reconciliation. (I couldn't tolerate having anyone mad at me.) He would say, "Could you just give me some time? I'm not finished being mad yet." We did follow the "Sun going down on your anger," Biblical teaching, but my husband needed more than 20 minutes to process his anger.*

Safe People do not say, *"That is just how I am"* *to justify using hurtful words.* When used, "That is just how I am," is an excuse to marginalize how rude or offensive one's behavior was. Saying that you are just being "honest" to verbally cross someone's boundaries is not safe behavior. We are to speak the truth *in love.* This means that forethought, gentleness, and care for the other person are part of our motivation. If a loved one refuses to own this behavior, we get to choose and perhaps limit our contact with them for our own good. Remember, that love is choosing for a loved one's highest good. This begins first and foremost with choosing for our own highest good. We are called to love ourselves.

Safe People tell the truth...in love. They are brave enough and care enough to be honest. When the conversation may be difficult, they pray in advance, take their time, and communicate in a calm clear way.

Safe People respond rather than react. Reacting is when we are impulsive and led by our emotions in the way we reply to a situation. Whereas responding, is when there is self-awareness and forethought as we give ourselves time to think over our words and choices.

Sometimes we have no control and react instantly. If someone jumps out from behind a door, throws a surprise party for you, or pulls in front of you in traffic, you will react. Reactions can be instantaneous.

We respond to others when we give ourselves "think time" to choose our words. We allow ourselves time to gather information about what is happening. Paying attention to our negative emotions will help us to respond rather than react. When we begin to feel angry, irritated, or frustrated in a conversation, it is perfectly alright to tell the other person, "Give me a moment to think about this." Or "I need to think about this. I don't want to respond to you off the top of my head." We can give the other person an appointed time when we will come back to the matter. Much of our regret stems from the times we react in a verbally abusive way. This is usually the case when we react rather than respond to others.

*Safe People allow a person to not attend, go, or participate…*without punishing, guilting, manipulating, or cajoling. Yes, there is a time when our children, especially teens, prefer not to attend events with the family. There is a selfishness at this age and teens need to learn to value and participate in family events. Therefore, parents may compel their teen to attend and participate. But with adults, we may be disappointed and wish for the company of another, but we allow others the freedom of choosing whether they want to participate.

Safe People accept "I don't want to…" as a perfectly good reason. It is shocking how many people are not able to say, "I don't want to …" Is it okay to have wants that differ from someone else's and state them?

This is an interesting concept, especially between women. I only have one friend that I feel comfortable with saying that I don't want to go somewhere when invited. I can say, "No I don't want to meet for coffee, I am having an alone day," and it is okay. I have not mastered this one yet, and usually come up with an excuse, but I'm better than I was.

Safe People do not touch others unless appropriate and welcomed. Need I say more?

Safe People take responsibility for their choices. Many people blame others for triggering an angry or violent reaction. (See react vs. respond above.) An example, is someone blaming another for an action. "The reason they punched a hole in the wall with their fist, is because 'you made them so mad.'" To test if a person has the ability to choose control and needs to take personal responsibility, one only needs to ask themselves if this behavior would still happen if there were company at the house, or if they had a policeman watching them. If not, then the person has the ability to choose to control oneself.

Safe People do not repeatedly "dump" (I'm the victim) on others. If someone is always complaining about a spouse, child, job, or relationship and never takes action, they are not safe. I usually see these people sporadically and they are not intimate friends. They should not be in the inner circle of friendships. Many times, these individuals love to metaphorically puke all over others. They feel so much better after repeating the same sad tales of woe but leave others to carry the weight of their negativity. They refuse to own their power to choose their lives and, on some level, enjoy the attention of being the put-upon victim. (This will be discussed in detail in chapter 7.)

Safe People don't tell other people's confidences. Can you keep a secret? If you can't, say so. Trust is a big key to being an inner-circle person. Safe People do not delight in telling of other's shortcomings. Telling gossipy things that needn't be shared is often petty and possibly vindictive. It is a guaranteed way to never gain intimacy.

Safe People don't try to change others. Let's face it, if criticism actually worked, we would all be perfect by now. We have no power to change another. Thinking that if we just say the right words, someone will change is a fallacy. Remember, we can't change anyone but ourselves.

Safe People don't speak in "code." Speaking in code is where we expect someone to understand our non-verbal cues or inferences rather than just saying what we want or need. We often use this when we have trouble stating our needs. We all have needs and it is okay to state our needs. Let me tell you my code story.

Before we were married, Jeff and I were out running errands. As we were driving around one Saturday morning, I could feel my blood sugar dropping. So, I said, "Look, there is a MacDonald's." Jeff glanced, nodded, and kept on driving.

An hour later, I had a meltdown...can you say hangry? I began crying, saying I felt sick, and that my blood sugar was so low that I now had a headache and thought I might throw up.

Shocked and worried, Jeff asked me, "Why didn't you tell me?"

With tears streaming down my face, I accused him, "I did! I told you an hour ago that there was a McDonalds!"

To him, "There's a McDonalds," was an observation about a landmark. He didn't know this was code for, "Pull over immediately before I faint with hunger."

Why is it so hard to say, "I'm hungry?" Or "I need a hug." Or I just need you to listen without fixing me." Why does neediness feel so uncomfortable? Your needs are okay. They are okay with God too.

Safe People are willing to have others mad, sad, or disappointed with them. The truth sometimes hurts. Sometimes there are consequences for doing the unpopular, but right thing.

Safe People compromise. They want relationships over being right or having to always have their own way. We work *with* others to find win/win outcomes, rather than I win/you lose outcomes.

Safe People say they are sorry when they are wrong. This is part of the forgiveness walk of Christianity. We don't just go to God when we do something wrong, we go to the person we hurt too. When we sin against another person, we apologize…a real apology. Not an "I'm sorry if you felt that way" or "If I hurt you, I'm sorry." True apologies acknowledge the pain and hurt of what was done.

I am a believer that we model our faith for others. This is huge. Our preaching at, quoting scripture to, and criticizing others to try to change their behavior *DOES NOT WORK*. Actions speak louder than words. Probably one of the most powerful ways to show Jesus is in our weakness and humility. It is when we own our wrongs.

As a teacher in the public-school system, I was not allowed to mention the word Jesus, but I tried to model my faith all the time. Occasionally, I would lose my cool. I would be sarcastic, raise my voice, or embarrass a child. Upon reflection, I would know I needed to apologize.

I would call the child to the front of the room and I would say to the class, "I have called Johnny here because I want to say I am sorry to him for what I said yesterday. 'Johnny, I used harsh words and a mean tone to you yesterday when you continued talking. I am so sorry for that. I wanted you to stop but I was not patient. I should have given you a consequence, but instead I yelled at you and embarrassed you in front of the class. Since I embarrassed you in front of everyone, I am now saying I am sorry in front of everyone. It would not be right to just take you outside and speak privately when I did not speak to you privately yesterday. Johnny you are a wonderful kid and you do not deserve to be spoken to the way I spoke to you yesterday. You deserve to be spoken to with respect. Will you please forgive me?"'

I had to do this a handful of times per year. You could see the kids watch spell bound, mouths open, to hear an adult apologize in front of everyone. It was humbling for me, but I always felt I had just shown Jesus to them in a way I could never preach.

Apologizing is a tough thing. We, as Christians, are called to a higher standard, especially with our loved ones. When a conflict or disagreement arises, we are called to own 100% of our part; even if our part is only 5%...*REGARDLESS IF THE OTHER SIDE OWNS THEIR* 95%. We cannot do this without Christ in us.

Safe People talk disagreements out to an actual resolution. *They want a resolution over winning.* In so many families, there is conflict, the silent treatment, and then everyone pretends that everything is okay. There is never meaningful dialogue, mutual understanding, and true reconciliation. Furthermore, there is no intimacy and deepening of relationships. After conflict, we have to go back and discuss and clarify until there is understanding... even if that understanding is, we agree to disagree.

Safe People do not behave inappropriately to get another to behave appropriately. Parents, I'm talking about us. We can no longer scream and cuss to get our kids to stop screaming and cussing.

I used to stuff and stuff and stuff my frustration until I would shout the f-word at my children for arguing or fighting.

Or, how about the cleaning rampages, when I would throw their junk around screaming about their crap that's all over the house to get them to clean up?

Safe People stay on point. *They don't bring up previously resolved issues.* We don't try to "win" by dredging up all previous mistakes of another. Rather, we resolve the issue in front of us. If we have accepted an apology and forgiven a person, we give up our right to use that particular offense as ammo in future disagreements. We need to cast the memory of it into the sea of forgetfulness, just like God does with the sins He has forgiven us for.

Safe People isolate themselves when they are irrational. Notice I said themselves. When we are not fit for others because of a bad mood, or we are explosively angry, we separate and wait until we are calm and rational. We put ourselves in "time out" so to speak.

Safe People communicate with respect. Civility is the word. Beware of tone and sarcasm.

Safe People don't say the "WORST thing" to hurt the most. If someone didn't make the team or has an eating disorder you don't use this as fodder to hurt. When someone has shared their deepest pain, we don't violate that trust by using it in an argument.

Safe People don't threaten divorce or to end the relationship just because there is conflict. The most loving thing we can do for our children is to protect the marriage. Anytime the "D-word" is used, it shakes the foundation of marriage. We do not threaten divorce. Ever!

Moving Forward

As we begin down the path of becoming a safer person, we learn to let go. We learn to give up our rights to be understood, accepted, liked and validated. We don't speak the truth only when the outcome is going to be lovely, affirming and uplifting; we speak it because it matters. For some of us, this is where we pick up the cross and follow Him. Remember, we can't change our entire family in an instant. Rather, we begin our trek by asking God to help us change. We pray and ask for healing.

We can only behave in a safe way when we feel safe and secure. We live from the safety of knowing our identity in Christ. When we know we are accepted and loved, we no longer need external validation and we begin to see the validity in giving up our rights. This enables us to live and relate from a place of love and grace… God's highest good.

Family and relational dynamics will change as we educate our loved ones as to why *WE* are changing. There will now be transparency. And with our change in behavior toward love and what's best for our loved ones, we will need to take one more step, one more *BIG* step. We will have to atone for our past behavior and we will have to learn to own our behavior going forward. Be prepared to offer "I'm sorry" and "please forgive me" over and over again.

Often, this process goes hand-in-hand with abandoning attempts to appease difficult family members. I pray for you to be brave and to have courage, because it will get worse before it gets better.

Why will it get worse? Speaking the truth in love causes people to confront themselves. And let's be honest, people are demanding, difficult, angry, and disrespectful because on some level, it works for them. They may be repeating family patterns and living out of their unhealed family belief grid. They have their "roles," and speaking the truth is changing the rules or dynamics one has lived with up to this point. The appeased or dysfunctional family member is getting a desired pay off from the family dynamic. There will be a time of testing where the negative traits escalate. We are tested by others so they can figure out if this is real change. Expect it. Call it out in your own mind when it happens, and then stay the course. Your families will become healthier and you will be the catalyst for change.

Review of Tools:

Review last week's tools: *Walking Back Negative Emotions* and *Holding up a Hand*. Were you able to use them? Were they helpful? Share if you were able to use any of previously learned tools.

Tool # 7 - Assessing Safety and Intimacy

This chapter provides insight to assess who you should let close to you and who you should keep at a distance. When we think of boundaries, think about your property. Some people should not be in your yard at all. Some are safe enough to allow onto your front porch. Only a few get to come into your home. Only the absolute safest get to come into the intimacy of your heart/bedroom.

Questions for Discussion

1. Were any of the Traits of Safe People a revelation to you?

2. Were there any areas that you want to become safer?

3. Do you believe that everyone has the power within themselves to respond in a calm manner rather than to react impulsively?

4. Does your family resolve conflict to an actual resolution, or are you more likely to pretend that there was no conflict after giving the silent treatment?

5. Do you agree with the statement: We are called to own 100% of our part, even if our part is only 5%...REGARDLESS IF THE OTHER SIDE OWNS THEIR 95%?

6. What is a real apology? What is not?

ART CONNECTION

The Circles of Intimacy

Materials:

Various sized circles to trace. Consider using cups, bowls and cans.
Markers, Pens, Colored Pencils
8.5 by 11-inch sheet of paper (white)

Method: In this project you will place the significant people in your life into the circles of intimacy.

- Using markers, pens, or colored pencils, create a bullseye series of concentric circles.
- The innermost circle is you and the intimate place of your heart.
- Pray silently and ask God to help you place the significant people in your life within the bullseye you will create. Ask Him to show you if there are people who you allow to be in your inner circles who would be better kept at a distance.
- Place the names of your family or friends within the circles in relationship to how close they are to you.
- Where is God?
- Do you have any people in your life that are close to your innermost circle, but realize now that they should be more distant from you?
- Are there any people who should not be on the page at all?

Share, discuss, and pray if doing this in a small group setting.

CHAPTER 5

Codependency Matters

The Twisted Love of Codependency

What to Expect:

THE UNHEALTHY DYNAMICS ADDRESSED in this chapter is a result of families being out of balance. Understanding the behaviors of codependency and why we choose them, allows us to love our families better. We can then raise children who are independent from us and hopefully, dependent upon God.

Objectives:

In this lesson we will explore the following:

- Codependency has two strands, control and disregarding oneself.
- Codependency is learned in childhood and will repeat itself in families if not dealt with.
- Helping others is not always loving.
- Excessively helping your children undermines their ability to trust themselves.
- Suffering often draws us closer to God.

Twisted Love aka Codependency

Codependency is *excessive* emotional, psychological, or spiritual reliance on another person. Codependents can be either the relied upon person, aka the "hero," or the needy person, aka, the "rescuee." Codependency is like a dance which requires a minimum of two people. It is learned in our family systems as children and we carry it into our adult relationships. There are two parallel tracks of root causes within codependent individuals. On one side is the excessive need to control the outcomes of family members. This feels like love, and the intentions are to "help." On the other side, is a person who has not been able to mature to the point that they are able to love themselves or advocate in their own best interest. The following table models the two tracks and traits of codependents.

The Two Strands of Codependency	
Control	**Disregarding of One's Self**
Takes responsibility for loved ones' actions.	Acts without regard to one's personal needs.
Tries to change others to prevent potential "harm" or suffering.	Enables others to control them.
Doesn't respect boundaries.	Works toward earning approval.
Covers-up for the actions of others.	Puts more effort into another's problem than they do.
Manipulates others responses.	Lives life out of burden verses want.
Solves other's problems.	Needs to be needed.
Doesn't believe God is powerful.	Doesn't believe God cares.

One side of the codependency relational dynamic is rooted in fear, which manifests when one tries to control loved ones. On the other side is shame. The shame of the past has caused some codependent people to lose the essence of who they are, what they want, and how they want to be valued. They feel their role is to meet the needs of others. Because of the resultant control and/or low self-esteem issues, codependent people often feel safe in a dysfunctional relationship. Most codependent people are consumed with focus on *other* people in their life. Many codependent people seek to control or relinquish control in their relationships because of a broken relationship with God.

What Does it Look Like from the Inside?

It is easier to spot codependency in others, than to self-diagnose it. We can look inside our heart to see if we recognize any of the actions listed in the Fear-Based/Shame-Based Codependency chart below. You may not necessarily feel fear or shame, but you might recognize some of its results. Often people who struggle with codependency have both shame and fear as root causes of their choices.

Fear-Based Codependency	Shame-Based Codependency
Continually second-guessing decisions. Needing to make the "perfect" or "best" decisions.	Not knowing how you feel.
Agonizing over potential confrontations and then choosing to say nothing.	Lacking trust in yourself/poor self-esteem. Often talks oneself out of how they feel.
Feeling terribly upset when you think someone is unhappy with you or you have made someone mad.	Giving of yourself to others even when it hurts, exhausts, or limits you.
Living in your head, thinking about, and analyzing choices.	Hides vulnerability and when one does open up, beats oneself up for being stupid after sharing oneself. (timidity)
Feeling like something that is happening to a loved one is happening to you.	Calls attention to oneself in a flamboyant way (exhibitionism)
Feeling anxious about the decisions and possible choices of others. Being in your head on their behalf.	Not knowing what you want or desire except to please others.

Behaviors and Beliefs

We become overly responsible. Codependents tend to spend their time thinking about other people or relationships. Fear causes us to become obsessed when we might, or we have, made a mistake. Obsessive thoughts take over if it appears something painful or harmful might befall a loved one. This causes us to continually live in our heads rather than living in the moment. It steals the beauty and joy of life. Rather than living the present-tense life we are in; we live a theoretical life of imagining worst-case scenarios and how we might anticipate and prevent them. Acknowledging that we have little control over our loved ones, frightens us. So, we live hypervigilant lives full of anxiety.

We become an enabler. Our loved ones might have habitual sins that God might want to reveal and heal, but we prevent our loved ones from suffering the natural consequences of their actions. This is most apparent when someone continually covers for or enables an addict to escape the consequences of his choices. Sometimes we are purposefully oblivious, aka, in denial. We choose to ignore common denominators in relational situations.

- There might be repeated offenses that occur when someone is drinking which are ignored.
- Or year after year, teachers might "pick on" my child and it never occurs to me that perhaps my darling is disrespectful or a behavior problem.
- There might be drama with friends and somehow the fact that my child is in the middle of it each time is never an issue.

We become a caretaker. Codependence with a loved one who has an addiction is a slippery slope. The more we "care," the easier and deeper the addiction becomes. Codependents work hard to ensure their loved ones avoid the negative consequences for their actions…

the very consequences that might drive their loved ones toward healthy change. Sometimes our "caring" may look like cleaning up after violent outbursts. We may lie to our alcoholic loved one's place of work when he is absent. We might lie about money problems to cover up for a gambling problem. The list is infinite.

We become fearful/helpless. Sometimes, repetitive types of conflict happen involving loved ones, and rather than confronting character flaws or what is behind the conflict, we pretend that there is no issue. We deny the patterns right in front of us. We deny because we feel overwhelmed by our helplessness to resolve anything. Deep in our hearts we know we are inadequate to solve another person's problem, so we pretend there is no problem in the first place.

We feel flawed and unworthy. Neediness feels scary. We need to be in control, so we don't acknowledge our vulnerability and need for love and intimacy. We play games with loved ones, and it feels dangerous to admit weaknesses. Just saying outright that we need to be held by our spouse feels too intimate. We love to help others but hate, hate, hate when we need help. We would rather walk to pick up our vehicle than ask for a ride to the auto shop. Underneath all of this is often unhealed shame and trauma, which causes us to feel defective in our innermost being.

We become people-pleasers. "What will people think?" drives many of our choices. We need to make *EVERYONE* happy and not doing so causes us much anxiety. It almost feels like a sin if we make someone unhappy or have to say "no" and disappoint someone. We *NEED* people to like us.

We assume another's guilt/pain. Learning to detach is difficult. We often live in the confusion of "transference" of pain or anxiety from others. Transference is where we connect someone else's situation to something in our life. The pain and trouble our loved ones' experience *feel* like it is happening to us. We pick up the emotions of what is happening to others as though it were happening to us.

We struggle with boundaries. Bossiness and telling others what to do is normal to us. We might call this leadership, but at times we cross boundaries. We need to control the outcomes of others to feel okay.

We struggle in our relationship with God. And underneath all of this is a common denominator, a lack of spiritual trust where:

- We don't believe God is good.
- We don't believe that He has good plans not to harm us.
- We don't believe God is a good provider.
- We don't believe that God's approval of us is enough to define our worth.
- We don't believe that He would "withhold no good thing" from us.
- We don't believe that He loves our families.
- We don't believe He would act powerfully on behalf of those we love.

Causes

Children of divorce – These children feel guilt and inadvertently carry misplaced blame. Financial, emotional, and relational security is shaken or even shattered. Trust in the bonds and promises of adults is now suspect. Sick relational dynamics often enter in at this time as children are used as pawns between the parents. Sometimes the child becomes the caretaker when a parent shares adult worries and therefore burdens little shoulders.

Abused children and children of domestic violence – These children always blame themselves and feel responsible for the abuse is some way. They may go on to struggle with boundaries and live full of worry as they analyze choices to protect others from potential harm. Most harmful of all, is that the child comes to believe that at their core they are defective and unworthy of love. The only remedy for this, is learning that the Highest of the High, God…a greater authority than their parents, says they are worthy and loveable. It will take years for this to sink into the heart...but once we belong to Him it *WILL* sink in.

Children of addicted parents – These children become little caretakers. They feel responsible and will struggle with the "control side", as well as the "disregarding one's own needs" side of codependency. They assume responsibility at a young age for something that is not, and should not, be their responsibility. Therefore, until God and healing intervene, they will go on to assume the responsibility of caretaking, even when it is not in their personal best interest.

Children with a narcissistic parent – These children are gaslighted. They are required to place the needs of the parent above their own. If they speak up about their own issues, they are perceived as selfish. Trusting oneself is very difficult after growing up in this. They may have been rewarded or deemed to have value, when they were caretaking the narcissistic adult. This often carries over into caretaking, even to the point of self-harm in adulthood.

Children of the chronically ill/caretaker – These children will grow up trying to be "need meters." As they mature, they will have trouble receiving help from others while trying to control outcomes.

How We Inadvertently Carry It Forward

Most of our intentions for our loved ones are so pure, so good, so kind. We wish them success in every endeavor. We want them to feel loved. Loved by us, loved by God, and to love themselves. We want them to have prosperous lives with wealth, health, hope, and deep faith. We believe that this desire will come to fruition faster with our assistances. However, is being overly involved with our loved ones truly beneficial? That is, truly for their highest good?

It is time to point out that entire books have been written about each of the traits mentioned above. I could go on to write in detail about enmeshment, addiction, enabling, and spousal abuse to name a few. Those subjects, however, are not my focus. In the rest of the chapter, the focus will be on the effects of fear-based control and how that affects children and their future. I have been blessed with much healing for my control issues. I only have my little piece of the puzzle to share. Sharing my perspective will help those who have children and those who are involved with child-rearing. Anyone who struggles with control issues will find help here, even though the examples will be focused on parenting. The tools at the end of the chapter are applicable for any type of codependency and dysfunction.

When we hold our little babies for the first time, we are vulnerable in a way we have never been vulnerable before. The world now has a new way to destroy us; hurt our baby, hurt us. A deep bonding happens, and we become lions of love. We are fierce. We will walk through fire, fend off every attack from people and the world. Our feelings toward these little ones is how Jesus must have felt for us...I would die for this little one.

This distortion called codependency happens because we are *not* Jesus. We are not the Savior. We are not the superhero of our loved one's stories; *HE IS*.

Is all Helping Bad?

Regarding this unhealthy love, I call codependency, I just feel led right now to be clear, I am not saying that God never wants us to help anyone. That would be crazy. Of course, we are to help, serve, encourage, and be there for others. That is one of the fruits of the Spirit and a normal way the Holy Spirit moves to demonstrate the Love of God to the world.

The kind of unhealthy helping I am speaking of will have a pattern to it and it will not be for a loved one's highest good. There will be a negative relational dynamic of dependence on someone in an unhealthy way. Patterns are good indicators to pray about and consider. For example:

> *When my father died, I inherited a small amount of money. I wanted to do good with it, so I planned on giving it away. God had not yet taught me about loving myself, and I had a real problem with receiving. I thought God would love me more if I gave it away. I met a woman at church who was having car troubles, so I gave her some money to make a*

major car repair. (Super Chris to the rescue!) A month later she called me because she could not pay her bills. I paid them for her. Two months later, she called because she was struggling with her rent. At this point I got it. There was a pattern and I stopped rescuing her.

It wasn't until the third time this woman needed me that I even prayed about it. We all have to pray about our helping and examine the issue of control. Revelations about our motivations behind helping others are important factors in discerning if we should step in or not.

The Cure

Getting rid of codependent behaviors is a journey. Liken this process to a zealous superhero, struggling to go off duty. We are *all* learning to lay down our capes as our children transition from babies to adulthood. Babies need their parents to be in complete control. Toddlers *need* parents to direct everything. As children mature, they need less and less. There is a weaning away of "mother knows best" to where we are supposed to become our children's cheerleader, on the sidelines of their life, encouraging them as they make decisions. We are not to be their life coach. God is supposed to have this role.

To find a cure it is imperative that we look at the "*WHY*" behind codependency. Why is it so difficult to stop controlling others, to not give advice? Why is there this struggle of living continually in our heads as we try to figure out the right choices and paths for those we love? Why do we live in "convincing mode," believing that we know what others should do? Why do we carry the burden of our loved one's problems? Why do we cover-up to protect them from poor choices? We work so hard to convince and manipulate those we love into doing what we believe is best for them.

This struggle is related to faith and trust. Time is needed to build a deep, trusting, relationship with God. As we learn to have a relationship with God, we are encouraged to surrender our fears to Him. We also try to believe and receive God's truths regarding our worthiness. At first, this is extremely difficult, because He has no track record with us. As new believers, we are not sure that He will come through for us, especially since we may have many disappointments from our past.

Surrendering and trust usually have to do with unhealed issues within our hearts. It all goes back to the deep belief systems from our family grid, vows we took after experiencing pain, and choices we made to care for ourselves. After all, if we have no relationship with God, we only have our own power to protect us from pain. Relying on, or utilizing our own power to direct our lives, is the definition of control.

The Bible states, "As a man believes in his heart so is, he." (Proverbs 23:7) Because we have not had a deep relationship with God over a long period of time, we don't truly trust God. So, we try to trust in and rely upon ourselves. Underneath it all is a deep fear. We might not even be actively aware of the fear, but the struggle to let go, proves the point.

Codependency is prevalent when we don't believe that God is good, and that He is powerful. No condemnation here please! None of us believe that He is Good or Powerful all the time. The more devastation we have experienced in our home of origin, the more difficult it is to truly believe that goodness and power are true character traits of God.

So, once again, *IF* underneath it all, deep in the crevices of your heart, you don't believe that God is good or powerful, who does everything depend on? *It depends on you.* If everything…a loved one's safety, spirituality, success, depends on you; then you better be giving some good advice. In this twisted love I am calling codependency, we *MUST* help our loved ones to be okay. It seems loving. *WE CARE!* What is wrong with caring?

This isn't about caring. We will always care, and this feeling of loving and caring is from God. To cure codependency, we need to change what caring looks like.

Caring

Studying God's ways, His perspective, and His Highest Good for our loved ones, enables us to let go. Caring now looks like allowing our loved ones to find God for themselves. Caring for our loved ones means that we *SEE* them and want them to be fully in love with God and fully embracing themselves.

Caring means we are not creating a "*Mini-Me*" who has faith exactly like ours. Caring means that we allow Jesus to be our loved one's Savior. The word "Savior" becomes a little tricky. For God to be Savior, there needs to be an awareness that one needs saving. "Needing saving" always involves suffering, and we hate suffering. "Time" and "Good" are components we struggle with in this process.

First, we humans do not have the ability to have a long-range perspective when it comes to time. We can't see how the verse "In all things God works for the good of those who love Him," (NIV Romans 8:28) will play out for our loved ones. Why do we even have this scripture? Because *all things* don't always seem good! S—t happens, it hits the fan, and we oh so want to fix it, fix it, fix it!

Caring now means we must actively resist stepping into what is not our problem…for the adults in our life…including our grown children. We are learning to *stay in our own lane*.

Suffering

A second problem we have, is that we don't have a Godly understanding of suffering. In fact, because suffering sometimes brings unbearable inner pain, we avoid it at all cost. We are like uneducated cavemen grunting our beliefs. Me, suffering Bad; happiness Good. We have little ability to view suffering from God's perspective.

> *Not only so, but we also glory in our sufferings, because we know that suffering produces perseverance; perseverance, character; and character, hope.*
> —Romans 5:3-4

This theme, that suffering is bad, and happiness is good, interferes with coming to faith in Christ and having a deep relationship with God. Intervening in the lives of others, getting into their lane, refusing to allow another to experience the consequences of their choices can be extremely selfish and *is not loving*.

> *It was a rude awakening when God began dealing with me on this issue. I was so attached to my children, that their suffering felt like it was happening to me. There was an unhealthy, twisted, enmeshment going on, to which I was completely oblivious. Underneath all my helpfulness, was a drive for ME to avoid suffering. If my family suffers,*

I feel it, and so I mowed down every possible obstacle in front of my children whenever possible.

"I'm not being selfish, I'm helping!" is the codependent's indignant cry. Isn't helping someone good? Let's think back to our definition of Love…*Behaving, speaking, and responding on behalf of another for their highest good or for their long-term benefit.* Our absolute highest good, is having Jesus. This love relationship with God then enables us to love ourselves and love others.

Building Confidence

Sometimes when we "help" others, we are robbing them of the opportunity to respect and value themselves. Our need to be the hero can be selfish. It feels good to be helpful, to be bragged about, to be wise and all knowing. It feels great to get that pat on the back for helping someone solve a problem. I liken it though, to that smart kid who always blurts out the answer in class. When a child does this, he is robbing another student of the opportunity and the joy of learning. When we automatically step in to help rather than encourage and cheerlead, we are robbing our kids of growth and learning.

Excessively helping your children erodes their confidence. My being "Mommy on the spot" had eroded their confidence in their own abilities.

I had good intentions, but I was misinformed. As a teacher in the 1980s, I became certified during the self-esteem movement. I was taught that children have a low self-image because they lack confidence and self-appreciation. To remedy this, I was to notice all the good things that they were doing, acknowledge them, and give compliments…. lots of praise and compliments.

Now, I have nothing against praise and compliments. We all need them, and no one loves a good compliment more than me. The problem is that giving excessive praise and compliments does not build confidence. It does not build character, or strength, or problem-solving abilities, or trust in oneself. Sort of like "Participation Trophies" don't build team character, strength, or confidence...

These things: confidence, strength, character, trust in oneself and problem-solving abilities are built *in fear*. Yes, you heard me right, *in fear*. Not running from fear, but doing something in the midst of fear...feeling fear but doing something anyway.

When we do something in the midst of fear, there is learning and usually success. It never goes as badly as we imagined. We surprise ourselves and do better than we expected. We do this over and over again, and we become brave. We become confident. We become fearless. We learn that we can trust God, ourselves, and the abilities He placed within us. We come to understand that God and self are enough. We come to appreciate the gifts and abilities He *placed* within us. He created each of us unique and different and He is most fully glorified when we are most truly ourselves, embracing our gifts.

Recognizing We are at Fault

When we "help" our children with school projects, friendships, acquiring or paying for things, speaking on their behalf, setting appointments, providing them money so they don't have to work; we are communicating an unintentional, harmful, underlying message.

What we are inadvertently communicating is: "You are weak. I don't believe in you. You really don't have what it takes in life. And without me to help you, you can't survive." No mother would say these things to her children, but actions speak louder than words. So, not only are we fostering a broken, codependent relationship, but we are unintentionally giving our children low self-esteem! A counter point to this is seen in the military.

The making of a soldier models building confidence in the midst of fear. Have you ever had the experience of dropping off a family member at boot camp? We kiss them good-bye, and the next time we see them they are a mature man/woman. Boot camp is all about facing fear. Those young people face test after test of what seems to be impossible feats. Some days they are successful, some days less so. But they always surprise themselves. All are broken. In this brokenness, they reach out to their classmates and build authentic relationships. They learn that there is a Savior, ideally Jesus, and worst case their Drill Sergeant. The worst happens and they are okay. They come out capable and confident men and women. And all of this happened without our intervention.

Connecting the Dots

Now let's connect the dots. When do people seek God? When do people have seasons of deepening their understanding and receiving from God? Is it when we are at Disney World or a hospital? Is it in acceptance or rejection? Is it in abundance or in need?

If God's greatest good for my children is that they have their own deep, authentic relationship with Him, then they need some trials and chances for God to show up. Codependency, "helpful" interference, hinders that process.

I do not devise what I am writing out of theory, but out of experience. On this pathway to understanding, I faced almost paralyzing anxiety. My children went through the kind of personal brokenness where you as a parent feel like you are dying. The kind of torment when you fear for their lives, health, and any hope of a bright future.

During this time, both of my children were adults in their early 20's. I was also completely, totally, and devastatingly aware, that pushing my faith had actually eroded theirs. Why? Because of crossing their spiritual boundaries When my children were small, I was the "Junior Holy Spirit." I wanted them to have faith and took seriously the scripture about teaching your children the way they should go. But finger pointing and using God's name to try to create "Godly" children, turned them off to Jesus.

My daughter told me during this time, that she didn't understand it, "But every time I mentioned the word Jesus, she wanted to scream." Not a proud truth and diametrically opposed to my intention.

So, here are my shattered children and I am wrecked. I know that anything I say spiritually will drive them further away. At the time I most wanted to intervene, I am unable to do so. I know that the way I used God to parent, and the way that I loved, is twisted. It won't work anymore. I am compelled to release, pray, and trust God. And guess what? God showed up. For both of my children. Through this season of their personal suffering, I laid down my cape and God saved them. In their need, they sought Him for their own selves, and He came through for them. God *LOVES* our children, especially when we get out of His way and let Him.

Conclusion

Healing from codependency is a process that we embrace even though it feels scary. We feel afraid for our loved ones. We fear letting go because we are afraid God won't come through for those we love. It is best to recognize the fear and say what is *MOST True*. It is true that I feel afraid that if I don't _____, something bad might happen, but what is *MOST True*, is that God is good and God is powerful.

Review of Tools:

Review last week's tool: *Assessing Safety and Intimacy*. Were you able to use it? Was it helpful? Share if you were able to use any of previously learned tools.

Tool # 8 - Becoming a Cheerleader

We must resist helping. We encourage independence from us and dependence on God. Encouragement now comes in the form of affirmation of the innate wisdom and problem-solving ability God put in each of us. Below are some of the new ways we allow our loved ones to grow. These are our cheers!

- Bummer, that sounds like a big problem. What are you going to do?
- I know you are so smart. How are you going to handle that?
- That is what I have always loved about you. You are smart and figure things out.

- Yikes, that sounds like a God-sized problem. How could He help you?
- What are you thinking is the right thing to do?
- Wow, that is a big one. Have you prayed about it?
- You make good decisions. I know you have what it takes to work through this.
- What am I giving you advise for? You are smart. What are you going to do?
- That is what I have always liked about you. Troubles come, but you and God work them out.
- You have a great brain. What is it telling you?
- What do you think your choices are in this?

Tool # 9 - Detaching

Detaching is unplugging from the feeling that what is happening to someone else is happening to you.

- Simply saying aloud, "This is happening to _____. This is not happening to me," helps tremendously.
- Another way to detach, is to ask yourself if you are the main character if this were a story. If not, we say aloud, "This is not my lane, nor my problem. I love _____ enough to *let them have* problems and to *figure out* those problems. I love them enough to allow them to have their own God story."
- Visualizing your loved one as tiny, as a child in God's hand, and you far away helps with detachment. It is also beneficial to see yourself little. Visualize yourself little and then jump onto God's lap. Maybe you see your loved one as little too, sitting on God's other knee. It is extremely comforting to embrace

the reality of our littleness and it helps with detachment. My absolute favorite Bible verse of all time is:

My grace is sufficient for My power is made perfect in weakness.

—2 Corinthians 12:9 NIV

Questions for Discussion

1. Do you see yourself on one side or the other of the root cause of codependency: either control or disregarding yourself?

2. Do you ever feel like a family member's problems are happening to you?

3. Who is the "hero" in your family and why?

4. Do you agree that excessively helping your child can undermine their confidence?

5. Tell about a time you did something even though you felt afraid. What happened?

6. Tell about a time where you grew deeply in your faith. Was it in a time of suffering?

ART CONNECTION

Laying Down our Capes

Materials:

Cape: Large sheet of butcher paper or the back of wrapping paper. (About 2 by 3-foot per person)
A Cross, either symbolic or real.
Markers
String or yarn for necktie

Method: This lesson will help to reveal who you are codependent with in your family. You will be provided with the opportunity to process who you help in an excessive way and why. You will also have the chance to surrender your loved one to God.

- If the technology is available listen to this song on You Tube: Steffany Gretzinger, *Save Me* with lyrics.
- Pray and ask the Holy Spirit if there are people in your life that you are involved with in an unhealthy and overly controlling way. Ask Him to show you who and how you are trying to save or help this person or people. Is there someone that you help, even though it is harmful to you in some way?
- Ask God to give you the will, the faith, and the power to surrender this person or people to Him. Ask Him what you need to give up or let go of. Sit silently and allow God to speak to or inspire you. Then create a super-hero cape.
- On this cape, list who you are loving in an unhealthy and

controlling way. Name the ways that you most often intervene in one or two-word phrases.

- If time allows, put on your cape as you discuss why you made your cape the way you did. If doing this independently, meditate on your creation in prayer.
- When you feel led, come, and lay this cape at the feet of the cross. Or if you have a real cross, nail it to the cross. Ask God to forgive you for trying to be the savior to your loved ones. Tell Him that even though it is difficult to trust at times, you are letting go and asking Him to be the Superhero of your loved ones' stories.

Share and discuss what you surrendered to the cross with your group. Pray for one another.

CHAPTER 6

Healthy Matters

Healthy vs. Unhealthy Families

What to Expect:

OUR FAMILIES SEEM NORMAL to us. Therefore, it is easier to discover if our families need healing in a particular area by broadly exploring various types of family dynamics. Think of the chapter ahead as a doctor's checkup. There will be areas of health to celebrate and some areas that might need change to be healed.

Objectives:

In this lesson we will explore the following:

- Healthy families are able to solve conflicts in respectful ways.
- By speaking the truth in love, we grow mature adults.
- Unhealthy families often insist their family engage with toxic family members because of the hope/fantasy that the toxic individual will change.
- Appeasing is not loving.
- The "Don't Talk Rule" is used to shut down honest communication.

Healthy Families

The healthiest families have clearly defined roles with immediate and extended family. We love one another and that is evident in our communication, behavior, and respect for boundaries. We communicate in safe ways that build healthy relationships. In relationships that function well, family members share common goals and work as a team.

The single most important trait in healthy family systems as opposed to unhealthy family systems is how interpersonal conflict and negative circumstances are handled. Somehow healthy families are able to be honest and confront in a way that is truthful but does not end the relationship. There is an aim towards using the appropriate tone of voice, and a willingness of both sides to hear and discuss negative or disagreeable issues, even when one feels criticized.

Tone of voice is a big indicator of health versus dysfunction in families. Respectful language and tone are the norm in healthier families. The adults should model respectful language toward other adults as well as towards the children. Or as my mother used to say, "Healthy families do not speak kindlier to strangers on the street than they do to their own families." Yes, at times there is anger, yelling, and withdrawal, but these behaviors are owned and overcome. For the most part, the parties involved want to understand, negotiate, and find the middle ground.

Then we will no longer be infants, tossed back and forth by the waves, and blown here and there by every wind of teaching and by the cunning and craftiness of people in their deceitful scheming. Instead, speaking the truth in love, we will grow to become in every respect the mature body of Him who is the head, that is Christ. From Him the whole body, joined and held together by every supporting ligament, grows, and builds itself up in love, as each part does its work.

—Ephesians 4:14-16 NIV

Speaking truthfully to one another in a loving way is key to developing a mature family system where each member fulfills his or her appointed part. Truth speaking and truth hearing enhances our ability to mature in our faith. When truth is not allowed to be spoken, both spiritual and emotional growth and maturity are stunted.

Adults who come from dysfunctional family systems often lack basic understanding of what healthy family systems look like. Even when we understand that relational change needs to happen, we lack the tools to achieve the changes needed to heal our family relationships.

The greatest tool we have toward changing our relationships is *insight*. How and why is our system unhealthy in the first place? There are usually three relationship dynamics going on that cause us to avoid confronting something quickly and truthfully.

- We may insist our family join us in support of a fantasy relationship.
- There may be a difficult person in the family that everyone appeases.
- The "Don't Talk Rule" might be used to shut down honest communication.

Forced or Fantasy Relationships

Often, we insist that our immediate family interact with extended family who are unsafe or abusive. This is when one adult family member is not able to let go of an "ideal" of what they hoped for as a child; loving parents, close loving siblings, or children who respect others. Maybe they wanted a loving and supportive mother. Maybe they wanted a dad who would take an active part in their lives. These are good desires and not unreasonable. But there may be a disconnect between the desire and the reality of the relationship.

Sometimes family members are forced to engage with abuse, because a loved one cannot let go of this fantasy. This happens when the ideal of what a family "should" be is opposed to what actually is.

Some members of a family can be difficult to be around. They might be rude, disrespectful, abusive, or unkind. Because of the familial line, there is the perception that because someone is "family," everyone has to be in a relationship with this person.

We don't want to give up the fantasy that we have a loving sister, or a caring supportive mother, or a kind aunt. Instead, we keep showing up and insisting our family members show up, only to be mistreated, unappreciated, or abused. We keep hoping that "this time" it will be different, only to be disappointed. It is sad that not only do we show up for abuse, but we demand our loved ones join in the charade so we can have our fantasies.

When we try to speak the truth in love about the abusive person, we are shut down. Usually, the "blood" or DNA connection is used. Blood ties are said to be more important than the way loved ones are being treated. Often, when we speak out about the toxic family member, we are shamed and accused of disloyalty to the family. Thus, honest dialogue is shut down. The abusive family member is allowed to be immature in their growth because they do not have to experience the consequences of their negative behavior.

God is not calling us to be in abusive relationships. He calls us to forgive, but not to show up or insist love ones show up to be hurt. Relationships are negotiated, and a two-way street. So, in healthy families, we allow our loved ones to choose their relationships.

Appeasing

Appeasing is the second dynamic that causes us to not speak truth-fully with our loved ones. Appeasing is where we feel like we have to walk on eggshells around particular individuals. The appeased may be a bully and take-out frustration on others. Or, we fear the emotions of our loved ones and believe it is our role to make them happy. The intent is good. Of course, we want to make our families happy. But sometimes this is out of balance. My insight into this began with a dream, a God dream.

> *My father was handing me a book, entitled* Boundaries: When to Say Yes, How to Say No to Take Control of Your Life. *It had a blue cover with white writing, and it was by Henry Cloud and John Townsend.*
>
> *Never having heard of this book, I wondered if it existed or if it was "just a dream." The librarian led me directly to the self-help section, and there it was. Talk about God promising to teach us directly. And so, I began to read.*
>
> *Honestly, the book overwhelmed me. Have you ever had the feeling that you are so emotionally screwed up that you start to think that you will never be okay? That is how I felt. Like, wow. I don't even know what I want other than*

to make everyone happy. If I don't even know, how can I choose? What does it mean to say, "Yes" and "No" if you don't even know what you actually want?

You might be thinking how can you, "not knowing what you want" have anything to do with speaking the truth in love? When we refuse to live from our hearts, our desires and wants, we live to please others. This results in us appeasing others. Appeasing is not loving. Remember our definition: *Love is speaking, behaving, and acting on behalf of another for their highest good.*

Appeasing means to pacify or placate. Think pacifier. You give a pacifier to keep the baby happy…to put it crudely…to shut the baby up. The result is immaturity with pouting, whining, and throwing fits when the appeased find their way thwarted.

Appeasing hinders the spiritual growth of the one being appeased because loved ones are never compelled to look at their selfishness or the motivations of their hearts. There is no accountability as to how words and demands truly affect others.

The appeased looks to the appeaser to be their need-meeter, their wish granter, and the one who comes through in times of trouble, rather than looking to God to meet their needs. Authentic relationships are hindered. We all have a deep desire to be known and loved by another. When we appease and pacify, we are "having peace when there is no peace."

They have also healed the hurt of My people slightly, Saying, 'Peace, peace!' When there is no peace.
—Jeremiah 6:14

Bitterness is the fruit of appeasing because if you do not have the ability to say "no" without there being some type of backlash, then you are not loving and giving freely.

Appeasing is not love. Appeasing is not for another's highest good.

The appeased, the difficult catered to family member, has a deep heart need for God. The appeased crave true love and relationships with others. These two things never get to develop because the counterfeit is settled for.

Have you ever been so thirsty and all that was available was soda? Or you are on a weekend trip when all that everyone eats is fast food meal, after fast food meal? When you finally get the water or that meal with grilled chicken and some vegetables, it is so perfect, so delicious. You realize that was what you craved all along. That is what it is like for those difficult, catered to individuals. They are craving God and deep relationships, but settle for the control of just having their demands met.

> ...*my whole being longs for you, in a dry and parched land where there is no water.*
> —Psalm 63:1 NIV

Is God big enough, loving enough and powerful enough to meet every need of a loved one? Can we love one another enough to learn about boundaries and respect them? Can we love ourselves enough to say no and make people angry if we really do not want to _____?

As we look at appeasing through the lens of love in terms of our definition of highest good, we can begin to change.

When we have patterns of intervening in the problems of our family, there is a trust issue with God. Having patterns of anxious thoughts over loved ones where we are stuck in worry, or something feels like it is happening to us, indicates we may need healing in our family relationships. More than that, it indicates we don't trust God.

One huge area of the conflict and frustration within our family systems is because one family member believes it is his or her job to fix problems, help everyone feel good, and to bring about happy outcomes for others. When someone believes they are the family fixer, they try to control others. Control is a huge problem, and it is not of God. Some might even say that it is evil. What? "Isn't that a bit extreme," you may be thinking?

Let me tell you, that I am preaching to myself here. I am a recovering control freak. I struggle with this daily. I am in the process of learning to believe that God is good, and God is powerful. We are all on this same journey. We have little power to change ourselves. We recognize our issues with control, and we ask God to change us.

So why the extreme statement...controlling others is evil? Controlling others violates the primary principle of Heaven. Choice. God could have created us and given Himself power to control us. We could have been like his adored pets, led around with a loving leash, but He chose to limit Himself. If we are *forced* to love someone, it is not love. We get to choose. We all hate being controlled, and if God Himself, who actually *KNOWS* what is best for us, won't control us, who are we to control others?

I know how difficult it is to give up controlling. That is why several chapters will be dedicated to this concept. Tools will be provided that will help us learn to let go, trust God and to help us deal with the anxiety that occurs when those we love are making destructive choices.

The Don't Talk Rule

Sometimes adults, or one particular adult in a family, are permitted to be angry, disrespectful, and volatile. They can express their negative emotions; while the other family members are expected to be respectful, controlled, and silent. There is a double standard at play. Adults can behave inappropriately, but everyone else is to behave appropriately. Any hints that the adult/adults made a mistake or were in error is quickly shut down.

The above double standard is an example of the "Don't Talk Rule." "The Don't Talk Rule," is employed when individuals do not want to hear, deal with, or process problems. When this is employed, the tables are turned and "Talking about the problem, becomes the problem," rather than the actual problem being the focus.

Think about the reality TV show called *Cheaters*. Every time that the "Cheater" is caught, the issue becomes, why didn't you talk to me in private? The issue/blame becomes the way the problem is being spoken about, rather than the betrayal, lies, and infidelity of the cheater.

When the "Don't Talk Rule" is in play, ploys are used to shift the dialogue. Instead of hearing and resolving, tactics are used to get the person who brought "it" up to be quiet. Anger, shouting above the voice of another, distraction, and withholding affection are the weapons used in the, "Don't Talk Rule."

- Anger - Dialogue is shut down when a person goes into a rant or tirade as soon as there is perceived criticism. The more timid family member withdraws, becomes silent, and communication stops.
- Talking over - We see this in arguments. One's point of view is

restated over and over again, until there is shouting. Whoever is the loudest "wins," but nothing is resolved.

- Distraction - Or the, "go into the offensive mode to defend yourself" play. This is when the problem is not the problem; the person bringing up a problem becomes the problem. For example, it is not that someone is drinking too much, it is that the person bringing it up is no fun or is judgmental. It is not that because a couple hasn't had sex in two weeks and there is an intimacy issue, it is that the person bringing it up is labeled as a sexaholic.

- Withdrawing affection - This is passive aggressiveness. We don't use our words, but our actions speak louder than words. When we give someone the silent treatment, slam cupboard doors, or storm out of the house; we are punishing others for criticism or perceive slights. It is like saying, "I won't be in a relationship with you if you talk about this." This is another tool to shut up any criticism and hinders resolving issues and healthy communication.

Our ability to speak honestly and to confront others matters. Being able to navigate difficult conversations is a skill, and is vital in forming and maintaining solid, loving relationships. Our intentions with our loved ones are good, but we may need to learn better ways to communicate during difficult times. We look back at patterns of communication. How were we allowed to express ourselves during confrontations as children? How did the adults in our life express themselves when they were distressed or upset?

Insight into the unhealthy family dynamics might feel painful at first. It feels uncomfortable, overwhelming, and even scary at times. If this is the case with you, it is because you believe that changing your family *DEPENDS* on you. That very belief is one of the reasons why we struggle in our relational dynamics in the first place. Thank God we are not that powerful!

We are little. We embrace our littleness, and it brings us comfort. We are the children of a great *BIG* powerful loving father. If there are any dynamics God is revealing, it is because God is speaking the truth to you in love. He loves us enough to reveal and heal us. He loves our loved ones the same way.

Review of Tools:

Review last week's tools: *Becoming a Cheerleader* and *Detaching*. Were you able to use them? Were they helpful? Share if you were able to use any of previously learned tools.

Tool # 10 – Surrender: Silent on the Outside, Praying on the Inside

The Bible teaches us the secret power of surrender and trust. It is a supreme act of faith when we refuse to control others and trust God to take action. This faith requires us to trust that God loves our families more than we do.

The kind of faith and surrender I am speaking about is not doing "nothing." Rather, we are silent on the outside and trusting on the inside. We aim to be at peace and may be quiet as far as words spoken aloud, but we are activating power. Inside we are not silent. Inside we are praying. Rather than thinking/fixing, thinking/fixing in our family systems; we are praying/releasing, praying/releasing…

Self-awareness is needed, as we resist directing and controlling. Instead, we send glancing prayers upward. These glancing prayers towards God are part of what the Bible calls abiding. He is *WITH* us. All it takes is a moment of directing our thoughts and hearts toward Him for us to become aware of His guidance.

When it comes to loving our families, we enter a silent and abiding dialogue… "God? Speak or be Silent?" "Intervene or let go?" …You *WILL* hear. You *WILL* have an urging or a checking feeling that will direct you. Instead of "US" telling others what they should and ought to do, we ask God to show them.

♥ *Little prayers like, "Thank you God for directing them." And "Please turn their hearts toward you. I know you love my family and want a relationship with them. Draw them to you in this situation." And then we let go.*

Questions for Discussion

1. What do you think the following means: Talking about the problem is never the problem the problem is the problem?

2. Assess the following statement: *You are God's creation, created to love and be loved. He says you have value simply because you are His creation.*

3. Do you agree that you have value simply because you are God's creation?

4. Tell about the fantasy you have had versus the reality of a relationship in your life.

5. What was your role in your family home? Give three labels that could be applied to you. I was the _____, _____, _____one.

6. Which family members were "appeasers" and which were emotionally volatile?

7. Is there someone in your life that you are appeasing? Do you know why you are doing this?

8. Complete this statement: My family loved me best when I _____.

9. Think about the "Don't Talk Rule." Is there a time that you or someone in your family used it to avoid talking about an issue? Share.

ART CONNECTION

Floor Plan of Your Childhood Home

Materials:

Crayons, markers, colored pencils
Rulers or a straight edge like the end of a book
8.5 by 11-inch sheet of paper

Method: This project will help you think about your family system and the roles of each individual. It will provide insight into the healthy or unhealthy family dynamics of specific family members and the way they related to one another.

After prayer, you will create a floor plan of your family home as a child. If you moved frequently, ask the Holy Spirit to show you one particular home to focus upon.

- Using the straight edge of a ruler or book, draw a floor plan.
- Place family members in the rooms. Where are they and why? Where is God? Where are you? Are there any labels or roles assigned?

Share with one another and discuss. Tell why you drew what you drew and why you placed each family member in that particular location. For some, memories might be foggy. This might be a bit painful. This is especially true if you had a difficult childhood. That is *OKAY*. Sometimes memories are hidden for our emotional and psychological protection. Just share what you can.

Ask one another questions. You may pass if you do not feel comfortable sharing.

CHAPTER 7

Choices Matter

Living as a Victim

What to Expect:

MOST VICTIMS DO NOT know they are living life as a victim. Their mindset is often obvious to those around them, but indiscernible to themselves. If we refuse to deal with the effects of being a victim, we will perpetuate two unhealthy dynamics into the next generation. We will either raise those who feel powerless and will view themselves as trapped when life brings negative circumstances; or we will raise children who have an entitlement mentality, who believe that their desires and needs are more important than others.

Objectives:

In this lesson we will explore the following:

- Victims believe that their wants, desires, and needs are secondary to others.
- There is a training process in dysfunctional families that teaches victims that they matter less than others.
- Every person has the same power to choose.

- Victims often refuse to own their power because they do not understand opportunity cost.
- Opportunity cost is the thing you give up to have the thing you want.
- Some people will never choose to heal from the victim mindset.

Introducing Victims

Let me confess, I am a daily reader of the Dear Abby column. I must not be the only one who enjoys this guilty pleasure because the advice column has been around for 64 years. What fascinates me is what people write about. The issues published allow us a peek into what troubles other Americans. If I could sum up the main idea of each question it amounts to something like this, "I am being treated poorly and my gut tells me to do _____ but I am not sure if I can trust myself. What should I do?" Or "I have a negative relationship dynamic in my life, and I feel powerless to change it. What should I do?" To many of us, the solutions seem so clear, but this is obviously not the case with those who write in.

Most of those who write in seem to view themselves as powerless. Like all victims, these writers seem to believe that their wants, needs, and desires are secondary…even when the wants and needs of others are harmful. Their choices are viewed through a grid that believes, "I must…", "I should…", and "I have to…." They seem to believe that they "must" be there for family members who are emotionally abusive. They "have" to be in a relationship with every relative, even those who hurt them or have hurt them in the past. They "should" make everyone at work like them. Victims believe they should: make people happy, bring peace, and be nice…that they should please everyone.

There is much blame assigned to victims. They are probably one of the most misunderstood people groups in our society. We are so, so, frustrated with them. Their power is within them. All they have to do is choose! What is so difficult about that?

Train: to teach (a person or animal) a particular skill or type of behavior through practice and instruction over a period of time.

Being Trained to be a Victim

When we come from abusive and extremely dysfunctional families, abusive behavior seems routine and par for the course. This causes us to be stunted in our maturity. The experience is normalized. And why not? Daily, routine, and repetitive patterns, are almost by definition the adjectives that define "normal." In many homes, it is normal for there to be explosive anger, physical violence, disrespectful language, and violation of emotional boundaries.

When dysfunction is normalized, a child's discernment is hampered. The ability to make choices for our own highest good is hindered. Wrong is said to be right and this distortion will affect us into adulthood. There is a deep ingrained training which happens over the years. It has to do with how we seek love, how we value ourselves, and what we can expect from those who say they love us.

Let me share a dream I had which demonstrates the dynamics in homes where this training happens.

In my dream were two tiny little girls, sisters, the size of Troll Dolls or a Polly Pocket. One lived in an underground pit with a metal grate over her head. The other one had a room in a small section of the family garage. It was warm enough, but she lived on the floor with a pile of blankets as her bed. It was normal for the girls to live like this, one in a pit and the other in a garage. It was understood that they would never grow to full size.

The family tossed food down to the girl in the pit, and she was brought out occasionally, if she was extra good. Her space was unclean and one of the reasons why, was because birds were allowed to perch over the grate above her and defecate on her. This was no big deal to anyone in her family. It was just the way things were.

In this dream I confronted the family. I confronted the father, the mother, and spoke to the children. I threatened to call Child Services but knew that they would not be able to effectively change the situation.

The family had no reaction to my outrage, but just pointed out the things they were providing. They had food. They were warm. The girls were tossed books to read if they wanted them. "See, everything is fine," was what they kept telling me. There was just complete indifference to the way the children were treated in the home.

I ended up snatching the sisters away from the parents. Neither the parents, nor the girls protested. The girls were allowed to leave at any time; it was no big deal. I just took the tiny, hand-sized girls, and we began a road trip.

On this trip, the girls did not need any amusements like coloring books or puzzles to keep them occupied in the car, just looking out the window and seeing the world from a whole new perspective was enough to absorb them completely. Just being out of the pit and garage was an adventure.

I awoke and knew it was a God dream and I began to pray for the interpretation. I believe this dream models the training process victims experience in their family systems, which teaches them to expect and live "choiceless" lives. One of the big revelations I got from this dream was the utter disregard and lack of insight from the family that anything was wrong. There was no recognition that abuse was happening, that it was wrong and needed changing. Even the girls were completely oblivious that things were off. Their life was just their normal.

The other revelation was that being continuously crapped on was totally fine. (Remember the birds?) To the girl it was normal, and to the family it was no big deal. Little "Tina" always gets crapped on. No biggie.

One of the most interesting patterns I have noticed with the women I teach is the lack of inner awareness of the abuse dynamic within their homes; that they grew up in a dysfunctional family system. They have been trained in the role of expecting less. They view dysfunction and abuse as normal.

So, so many times, I have heard women say, "I wasn't abused but...." Then after the but, goes on to say something that was totally abusive. Things like, "But pornography was available to me," "But my stepdad would sneak into my room and fondle me, but at least we never had intercourse," "But my uncle used to French kiss me," or "But my dad would have rages and we would all hide."

This negative training also entails looking at the "bright side." All the women preface any telling of childhood abuse with what they did have.... "They always provided for me," or "They paid for my college." "My parents took me to church." "Mama was kind...." They all tell of what they did have, but then go on to explain some type of devastation...the being crapped on so to speak.

Not the most holy of words, "crapped on," but a perfect description in the modern vernacular of what it is like to have been trained to be a victim. We have been trained to think of ourselves as victims because we *were* powerless. Children are powerless regarding roles in families. We had a particular role which caused us to help or cover for dysfunctional adults in our home. Our role was usually to please adults.

The desire to please adults translates to trying to make others happy in our current situations. There is an excessive need to be liked by our children, friends, and extended family. We become both the victim and the martyr. If feels like we have no choice but to live to please everyone, and then we hold resentment within our hearts. We live in constant fear, fear that we will not be able to make everyone content and satisfied. At the same time, we feel a bit peeved that no one noticed all our efforts to meet their needs and make them happy.

If we're lucky, as we become adults, we are awakened to what was wrong with our childhoods. We awaken to the fact that there were deep injustices in our homes. What we choose to do with this injustice is crucial to healing.

Recognizing the injustices of our young lives requires processing in our adulthood. We open our eyes to mistreatment, lack of love, and being taken advantage of. This processing is healing and a revelation. Our parents are knocked off their pedestals and we come to terms with our childhoods. We may feel disloyal for this. As we face the reality that though we may feel that our parents did their best; does not negate the fact that healing needs to happen. We embrace healing mode.

We learn to own our power. We learn to say what we want and what we need. This is something we must "practice." It does not come naturally. This process is just like being on crutches after an injury. You have learned to walk lop-sided. The way to healing is to activate unused muscles in new ways until we regain our balance and strength.

Victim training has caused us to live, feeling that if everyone is not happy with us, it is almost a sin. Now we are going to learn to do some very uncomfortable exercises. You know what they say at the gym, "No pain, no gain." The muscles we will activate are in our tongue, our lips, and our jaw. We learn to speak out for ourselves and teach others how to treat us. It can begin with four simple words. "I don't want to." This is where I started, and so can you...

> *"Mom, can you take me to Walmart right now?" a common request.*
> *"No," my answer.*
> *"Why not?"*
> *"I don't want to."*
> *Or...*
> *"Mom scratch my back." wheedling voice.*
> *"No."*
> *"Pleeasse!"*
> *"Why not?"*
> *"I don't want to."*

Shock and silence. Are moms allowed to say that?

Something so small and inconsequential, but powerful. "I don't want to." When we say these words, it takes away the "Why?" People ask us why so they can argue us out of our "No." When we give a "why," then they can push. They can begin to wear us down until we give up.

But by using "I don't want to," we are not manipulated into

putting the desires of others ahead of our own. These four words begin to break the entitlement mentality of those we love that expect us to place our wants beneath their wants. When you try this out, know that you will have to answer several "Whys?" with several "I don't want tos," over and over again. Often, the thing we are saying "I don't want to" to, is tiny, miniscule, and insignificant. Our loved ones will not be able to understand why we are suddenly changing the rules to something that is "No big deal." We stick to our guns because we are "practicing." We are doing an exercise to retrain ourselves from the victim mentality.

When we have dysfunctional pasts, we may think of ourselves as "less than." It even seems "Christiany" to serve everyone, and to put everyone else's needs, wants, and desires above our own. The big disconnect here, is that God does not call us to serve others in ways that will harm us personally, or stunt another's growth.

Let me tell you a story that models a sick love for one's children, a love that results in children believing we matter less than they do.

My friend, "Beth," shared a story about a particular Mother's Day when her children were teenagers. Her children woke up and when they came downstairs, they began to argue about where they would take her out to dinner. Their dad had left money since he was away working that weekend. There were no cards or flowers; the meal was to be the gift.

One of them wanted a steakhouse and the other wanted Mexican food. No one asked her where she wanted to go. So, Beth went upstairs, grabbed her keys, and headed to the Zoo. As she walked the exhibits, she contemplated how far the relationships had fallen from being celebrated with

*homemade cards and the "burnt toast" breakfast in bed, to
just being taken for granted.*

*Her children began to call and each time she would hang
up on them until they finally seemed to get it.*

"Mom what is wrong with you?"

"Wrong answer," click, she would reply.

"Mom, you are acting crazy," was next.

"Wrong again," click, was her next response.

*Finally, they got it, "Mom, we were selfish and showed no
appreciation this morning. You deserve more. We are sorry."*

This story really resonated with me, because I have had a Mother's
Day where I felt my family couldn't be bothered to recognize my
efforts to be a good mom. Yes, it is a commercial holiday, but we
love having a day when our sacrifices are noticed.

The story above sounds like Beth was a victim, a helpless unappreciated mom, but she is a player in the family dynamic. She was
living according to her training and training her children how to
view her and how to treat her. She had trained her family to think
less of her because she thought less of herself. Beth believed that
what they wanted, mattered more than what she wanted.

We who choose this path of living, "choicelessness," are at fault.
We have the exact same choices everyone else does. We *teach* people
how to treat us. Or as my mother says, "We get what we think we
deserve." We get what we put up with, whether it be at home, work,
church, or in our social relationships.

If you recognize yourself as one who celebrates everyone else, but
others do not celebrate you, you most likely have some healing to
do. God wants to heal your heart so that you love yourself enough

to believe that you deserve to be celebrated, loved, valued, and respected by others.

Staying Stuck, a Choice

Now for the really troubling part. Some of us will read this, see ourselves and embrace change. Some of us though, will be blind to our victim role and will continue to embrace choicelessness.

Victims of the victim mentality have the exact same choices that we all have. We all have the power to choose our lives, our people, and our circumstances. What victims don't understand is opportunity cost.

Opportunity cost is a concept I taught to my fifth graders in Social Studies. It is the thing you give up, to have the thing you want.

You can have an ice-cream every day, but you give up the X-box you could have saved for. You can go to college, but you give up the chance to earn money straight out of high school. You can get married, but you give up the complete freedom of being single. You can get a puppy, but you give up sleeping late in the morning, or having a pee-free carpet.

You can leave an abusive man, but you give up the security of his income. You can tell others the truth, but give up the right to have them happy with you. You can put up boundaries with unsafe people, but they will talk about you behind your back. You can stay in an abusive marriage, but your kids will be in abuse too.

Self-pity, or the "martyr syndrome," can be a pitfall for all of us who have had difficult childhoods. It keeps us stuck in victimhood. *Yes!* We *NEED* to tell our stories and process our pain and our past. We need to tell it more than once. Grieving and healing with a counselor or trusted friend is necessary. There is a point however, where retelling hurts us more than it helps.

Retelling can stir up self-pity and the pain we are trying to heal from. Haven't you experienced this? You had injustice done to you and you do the emotional work to get rid of bitterness, and unforgiveness. One day, you find yourself retelling the painful story and suddenly, all the bitterness, unforgiveness and anger are back full force. When we find ourselves retelling and retelling and retelling the same story, we must look at ourselves. Remember, Jesus asked the man at the pool, "Do you want to be made well?" If we are enjoying the attention of people feeling sorry for us, we might not want to be made well.

Living as a victim is the complete antithesis of the abundant life promised us as believers in Christ. The abundant life is freely given and is our inheritance because at Salvation we are now "In Christ." I am IN HIM and He is *IN* me! Scripture states, "It is for freedom that Christ *HAS SET YOU FREE.*"

> *It is for freedom that Christ has set us free. Stand firm, then, and do not let yourselves be burdened again by a yoke of slavery,*
>
> —Galatians 5:1 NIV

Slave or Free? We can now choose. Do we choose to live choiceless, powerless lives? Do we stay under the *"yoke of slavery,"* never healing from the generational beliefs and dynamics that were our childhood normal? Or do we practice making decisions and choices that are for our personal highest good?

What about Those Who Stay Stuck?

Sometimes we can get sucked into the misery and worry of trying to take care of someone who wants to be a victim. Victims often want to complain, but not make choices for change. This is perfectly okay. No one has to change. One can choose to stay in untenable situations. Life is not perfect and there is sometimes misery in relationships. But just as everyone gets to choose whether or not to change their circumstances, we get to choose how much we want to listen to the misery of their situation. If one is able to encourage and be helpful, we do so. If this is new pain, loss, or grief, we walk fully through the shadows with our loved ones.

Patterns, once again, are key. We need to look at patterns. Of course, God is compassionate, and we are too. We show our love by being there for someone when they are in difficult situations.

Hopefully, we are able to encourage those who see their circumstances through the lens of victimhood, to view or articulate their choices. After that, we must let go. We might share a story of a time we felt trapped and believed there was no way out, and that God showed us that we had choices. After that, the only thing I can suggest is prayer and detachment. We have no power to change others and need to protect our hearts from wallowing in someone else's pity party.

Let's face it, life is not always fair nor ideal. Jobs might suck. Bosses can be terrible. We go through difficulties, but we always have choices. There are times when we may be so hedged in that we feel like we have no choice. In these situations, we choose to pray and choose our attitude. This was the case of Viktor Frankl.

Viktor Frankl was a Jewish psychologist and a contemporary of Sigmund Freud. He spent three years in a Nazi concentration camp. He lost his wife, unborn child, father, mother, as well as his brother in the camps.

A remarkable man, he wrote the book, *Man's Search for Meaning* during a frenzied nine-day writing spree in 1948. During the evil and dark days of his captivity, he noticed that there were some individuals who were able to love and offer solace in the poverty and nothingness of the camps. His quote:

> *"Everything can be taken from a man but one thing: the last of the human freedoms - to choose one's attitude in any given set of circumstances, to choose one's own way."*

How remarkable. Viktor was a victim. His freedom of movement, choice of where to sleep, how to style or to even have his hair, the clothes he could wear, whether or not he had shoes, the opportunity to speak out, where to work, to be with his family, to protect those he loved…all were taken from him.

He realized and came to understand that no one could take away his beliefs. Despite oppression which few of us could even imagine, he did not stay stuck. He could have chosen to hate, and he could have chosen to live forever as a victim. Who would have blamed him? Instead, he used his power to choose hope.

My hope is, that like Viktor Frankl, we would choose to let go of our victimhood. We can and will choose to live our abundant life, a life full of choice, freedom, and hope.

Choosing Choice

You may be wondering what life will look like if you choose choice. To start with, you may save a life, especially if you have been allowing yourself to be abused. Fleeing is the hardest, and most necessary choice in the dire-most circumstances.

If you decide to stop living life as a victim, it will seem uncomfortable and feel selfish at first. You may even be told that you are selfish by your loved ones. Remember, that you are changing the rules in the family system and there is bound to be backlash. Slowly, you will begin to say "no" to those things you do not want to do. You will be doing less serving at church. You will be serving others less. You may even swing over into real selfishness for a while. But trust that you will swing back into Godly, spirit-led balance if you are seeking God in this process.

You will be healing from resentment. So much of what victims do causes resentment and bitterness in their hearts. Did you ever wonder why the Bible teaches to us to give cheerfully? Second Corinthians 9:7 states, "*Each man should give what he has decided in his heart to give, not reluctantly or under compulsion, for God loves a cheerful giver.*" When we give reluctantly or under compulsion, we feel resentment and bitterness. God wants us to live our lives out of "get to" rather than "have to."

Much of the service we do for the church and others is not because we are being called by God because of our gifting, it is because there is a perceived need we feel obligated to meet. Sometimes the worst jobs are delegated to victims. Victims will not refuse, because they hate to say no and they feel responsible to fill needs.

You will be doing soul searching during this process. You will be asking yourself, "What do I like?" "What do I prefer?" "What do I enjoy?" "What am I good at?" "What are my dreams?" 'What makes me feel alive?" You will be discovering the desires of your heart. You will be earning and receiving respect from family as they learn to view you with new eyes. You will be on your way to living the truly abundant life.

Review of Tools:

Review last week's tools: *Surrender: Silent on the Outside, Praying on the Inside.* Were you able to it? Was it helpful? Share if you were able to use any of previously learned tools.

Tool # 11 - Reframing

Reframing is rewording a situation that is a negative into a positive. It is like renewing your mind.
- Sample Thought - *My boss might be angry at me because I told him I could not take over all my co-worker's responsibilities during her maternity leave.* Reframe: *I am so proud of myself that I was able to speak up and get the help I need to cover for my coworker during her maternity leave. I have choices and I am loving myself by speaking up.*
- Sample Thought - *Oh no! My husband is upset that I refused to listen to him when he wouldn't stop shouting at me.* Reframe. *It is awesome that I am teaching my husband how to speak to me. I know he has the ability to control himself because I am the only person he speaks to in this way. This is backlash. It is uncomfortable, but this is good.*

Tool # 4 - Saying What is "Most True"

This is a good place to use Saying What is *Most True*. When we begin to make choices and own our power, our emotions can go haywire. It feels uncomfortable, wrong, and selfish. We can state the truth of how we feel, but then say the higher truth…what God says.

♥ *"God, it feels upsetting to have made my mother mad when I told her that she can no longer speak to me the way she has in the past. It is true that I feel like I am a bad daughter. But what is most true is that you love me and would never call me names. What is most true is you want me to love myself enough to speak up if I am being hurt in my relationships."*

Then, it might be helpful to use:

Tool # 2 - Giving Up Your Rights

♥ *"Lord, I give up my right to have my mother understand me and my new way of demanding respect in our relationship. You were not understood, and I won't be either."*

Questions for Discussion

1. Are there people in your life that you feel "You must…," You should…," or "You have to…?"

2. Do you agree that a person can be trained to feel like they have no choice in life?

3. Is there someone in your family system that is frequently given the short end of the stick (crapped on so to speak)?

4. Who in your family is spoken to with the least amount of respect?

5. Can you think of a situation when "opportunity cost" was a large factor in what you decided?

6. How often do you say, "I don't want to," to family members?

7. Do you celebrate others, yet they rarely celebrate you?

8. Is there someone in your life who enjoys a pity party, yet refuses to make choices for change?

ART CONNECTION

Choice Assessment Worksheet

Materials:

Pens or pencils
Copy of the "How Will I Make My Choice" worksheet

Method: This lesson will help you to walk through the process of decision making as we learn how to own our power to make choices.

- Pray and ask the Holy Spirit to illuminate a problem or conflict you experience in a family or friend relationship.
- Think about something that is troubling you within your family. Use the "How Will I Make My Choice?" worksheet below to practice analyzing problem solving.
- Come up with three possible solutions for your problem and a positive statement for each.
- Think about the opportunity cost of each possible choice. What will be the effect or the possible consequence of each choice? There may be more than one.

Finally, choose an option. Remember that we all have the power to choose.

Share your results with one another. Ask questions and pray.

How Will I Make My Choice?

Problem:

Solution 1	Solution 2	Solution 3
Positive 1	Positive 2	Positive 3
Opportunity Cost	Opportunity Cost	Opportunity Cost

My Choice:

CHAPTER 8

The Real You Matters

Authenticity and the Effects of Shame

What to Expect:

THIS CHAPTER IS ONE of restoration. In unhealthy family systems, we have learned ways to cope that protect the deepest parts of our heart. God's design is for us to live fully joyful lives. This means that we are restored to the deep places of our hearts. We learn to love and live more fully.

Authenticity: the quality of being authentic…of undisputed
origin; genuine.
Oxford Dictionaries, Oxford University Press

Objectives:

In this lesson we will explore the following:

- Shame blocks us from becoming our full self.
- Satan uses shame as children to lead us to paths of destruction.
- We most fully glorify God when we are most fully ourselves.
- God wants us to love and forgive ourselves.

Coming out of Hiding

It was my clear intent to bury this lesson deeply within this book. We first needed some tools, like understanding boundaries and safe people, before we could talk about shame. We have been hurt too often and for too long because we had no understanding of these concepts. If we talk about shame without providing an outlet of relief and tools for healing, it will be too overwhelming to process this part of our story.

There is a big problem with shame, and I personally believe this is Satan's most powerful tool to destroy us. Shame causes the "real" us to go underground out of a need for self-protection. This effects our relationship with others, with God, and with our own selves. We let our guard down when we unwittingly shared our "real" selves with unsafe people. Those experiences increased our pain, shame, and hiding. We were careless with our boundaries, who we trusted, and it exploded in our face. Now, by applying the concepts for healing in this book, we can examine shame from a point of safety and choice.

I can still hear the cry at the end of a summer's eve, "Come out, come out, wherever you are," as we played hide and seek with the neighborhood kids. We would hold our breath and try to be as still as possible so that not even an exhale would give us away. Afraid we might pee our pants, we held back the onslaught of fear while our stomachs dropped as the footsteps came toward us. Hiding, but also being found. The game wouldn't be fun if no one ever came to look for us.

I remember a different kind of hiding too, crawling underneath the family pool table in the dark garage. Remaining silent, wanting invisibility, my presence undiscovered as family came in and out to use the washing machine. Today, I don't even know why I did this, but suspect it had to do with shame.

We all hide. Of course, we do. Not every person is worthy of us. We have learned our lessons and learned them well. Hurt, betrayal, mockery, judgement; we are not stupid. People will hurt us physically, emotionally, or spiritually. One of our innate responses to danger is to hide or seek shelter. We also resist exposing ourselves to known danger. One of the definitions of insanity is repeating the same action over and over again, expecting a different result. We are not insane. The trouble with insulating ourselves from bad things is, we keep the safe and good out as well.

Shame always hides and causes silence. Behind this hiding is the belief that if I showed you this part of myself, I would be rejected. And this lesson is not about becoming Mr. or Mrs. TMI, that person who tells everything to everyone over and over again. The point is, you and I are living "robbed" if we do not deal with our shame.

The plan of the enemy has always been, "attack the children." The Bible tells of attempts to harm children. Even baby Jesus's earthly father, Joseph, had to flee with Him to Egypt to protect Him from being murdered.

Satan has a design to get us while we are young. If he can get us to doubt God's power and love, to hide and even hate ourselves as kids, then he is better able to lead us onto paths of destruction. Satan's grand plan is to sow pain and lies in our hearts. When he accomplishes this, he blocks us from growing to emotional maturity both in the natural and in the spiritual.

Shame causes us to reject ourselves and to hide. The "real us" goes underground and the imposter takes our place. Satan uses rejection by our friends and family to cause us to reject ourselves. We have no ability as children to sort out the logic of the pain and words spoken about us and to us. His design is always to use people to accomplish his goals.

Shame is pain, a deep inner pain in the core of our being. For many, the idea of facing it, or talking about it, is so overwhelming that it will remain hidden and silent until the day they die.

Shame lies silent and lurking, but influencing the direction of our lives. Rejection, self-hatred, loneliness, depression, and suicide are all a result of shame. The deep loneliness that accompanies shame hurts us. We can't tell the good from the bad, so often, we just choose to do life alone. Shame blocks us from fully developing deep, glorious love.

A Sidebar about God.

The character of God is glorious. There are not enough positive adjectives to describe God and His Glory. In fact, every positive attribute, character trait, or adjective that we humans can think of, originated in God and with God. *Every good thing comes from God* (para. James 1:17 NIV).

In the paragraphs ahead we are going to be thinking about glory, both God's Glory and our glory. Notice the use of uppercase letters in "God's Glory," yet lowercase in "our glory." This is a significant choice and an indication of my heart and purpose. I want to be clear that what I am going to speak about in the paragraphs ahead is not taking God's Glory for our glory. When we think of "our glory," we are simply recognizing and agreeing with God, that any beauty, value, or giftings we have are because He designed us.

God's Glory, Our Glory

We are meant to be glorious. Gloriously free, gloriously loving, gloriously generous, gloriously beautiful, and gloriously *UNIQUE*. We are meant to embrace the gifts God has given to us, including the gift of ourselves. Our own self is the only gift we can give to God. We give ourselves back to Him at Salvation. It is the *only* thing we have to give. It is also the gift we possess to share with one another.

We are each an individual gift to this world. We have people to connect with, jobs to do, creativity to express, words to be spoken… ways of loving *THAT ONLY WE CAN DO*. No one else is positioned in exactly the same way in their job, family, or friend dynamic than what you are right now. You have a sphere of influence that no one else has.

"What do you mean?" you may be thinking. Isn't it pretty presumptuous to think of myself as a gift to the world? This all has to do with Jesus. It is essential for you to realize how fully important you are to Him. To make this connection, I want you to think about something. Where is Jesus? And where are you from a spiritual point of view?

The Bible says that Jesus sits at the right-hand of the Father. Okay…we get this…. It says that we are *IN* Him. Crazy, incomprehensible, and mysterious, I know. And then it says that He is *IN* us. So somehow, we are seated with Christ at the right-hand of the father, and at the same time, Jesus is *IN* us, leading and guiding us as we walk the earth.

...it is by grace you have been saved. And God raised us up with Christ and seated us with Him in the heavenly realms in Christ Jesus, in order that in the coming ages He might show the incomparable riches of his grace, expressed in his kindness to us in Christ Jesus.

—Ephesian 2:5-7

To them God has chosen to make known among the Gentiles [those not of the Jewish faith] the glorious riches of this mystery, which is Christ in you, the hope of glory.

—Colossians 1:27

Now God could have created a mini-Jesus, one who perches on our shoulder whispering in our ears, like the cartoon angels and devils we saw as kids. He could have made Jesus an "App" on our smart phones that we could activate in times of trouble. God could have created Jesus to be like a fashion accessory, like a little suitcase or purse we carry around. "You got your Jesus with you?" someone may ask. And we could reply, "Yup, got Him right here," as we pat our backpack. We could carry Him around right next to us at all times.

But God did not do this. No, that is not Christianity. Jesus is *IN* us. Why? Why would God do something so crazy? I think it is because God is so vast, so extravagantly sublime, and multifaceted that it takes each created being and all the magnificence of creation to display Him, in His power, love, and glory.

God is continually displaying Himself through us. We are to be Jesus' feet, voice, and arms. Somehow, when God created us and led us to Himself, He found we were worthy of displaying Himself to the world in the uniqueness of "us." And the devil does everything he can to keep us from realizing this. This is why we have an epidemic of self-rejection. We do not love ourselves the way God intended. "God is for everyone else, but not for me," is often the theme of those who struggle. "I can forgive everyone else, but I just can't forgive myself," is our heart's cry when we are full of shame.

When we reject ourselves, we are rejecting God's love. Some might even label this refusal, to embrace and love ourselves, as prideful. The above thoughts are basically saying, "God, you died for everyone else, but I am just that one unworthy one. I just can't receive it." How ridiculous! Self-rejection and unforgiveness of oneself is like disregarding Christ's sacrifice on the cross.

When we begin to forgive and then love ourselves, it banishes shame and allows us to begin receiving the abundant life.

Notice the verb used above...*RECEIVE*. We can only receive this glorious, abundant life. There is no work, manipulation, or format to receiving from God. The abundant life is infinite and beyond comprehension. I am in process. You are in process. During this progression, layers of God's goodness and love for us are revealed.

The abundant life is summed up in one word, *LOVE*. Infinitely, continuing, endlessly receiving God's love. This love is then returned to God as we love Him. We are changed as we become grateful and hopeful.

LOVE for ourselves! It so blesses God when we begin to treasure ourselves, accept our quirks and bodies, and receive our unique, glorious splendor that He created when He made us.

Just as all of creation displays the glory of God; the ocean, the greenery and blossoms of a garden, a ladybug, the skies with ever-changing colors and vibrancy, so do we. We are created to display His glory. Did you know that God created over 350,000 species of beetles? Think about this...*Three-hundred-fifty-thousand types of beetles!* It appears that God likes variety.

Just as we can view the radiant splendor of a single stream of light that is visible through the clouds, each of us is an individual strand of radiance displaying God's goodness, creativity, splendor, and power. Even if we were somehow able to collect the cumulative weight of the beauty and magnificent variances of the body of Christ, it would be a minuscule reflection of our glorious God.

So, I want to present to you the idea that we most fully glorify God when we are most fully ourselves…our real true selves, in the unique way He created us. As a survivor of incest, trauma, and childhood sexual abuse, I have been on a journey of restoration. There are so many in the body of Christ who, like me, want healing from shame, blame, and self-hatred. We lack love for ourselves. The inner critic rules. The negative voices of shame, self-disgust, and that driving perfectionist, keeps us from receiving the self-love God has for us.

"Who cares about self-love?" you may ask. Aren't we called to love *others*? The trouble with not loving oneself is that one cannot give what one does not have. This is why we get stuck in unhealthy family dynamics. We are trying to give something that we do not have for ourselves. Until we begin to love ourselves, have compassion for ourselves, and have grace for ourselves, we are unable to truly offer those things to others.

We can now allow others to know the real us. We can begin to like ourselves. This process may feel like we are Sleeping Beauty, and we are being awakened from a long sleep. We wake up in the arms of our beloved God. We are safe, loved, and being sent out to love others. The question is, how can we do this in the midst of our unhealthy family dynamics? It begins with forgiveness.

Forgiving

Choosing forgiveness is the first precept of our faith. Every human has the same choice. We can ask God for forgiveness or we can live independently trying to rely of our personal merit with the hope that "being a good person" will be enough to earn eternal rewards. Just because there are worse people out there than me, does not negate all the wrongs I have done in my life. From the perspective of the pure, holy, and perfect love of God, I choose to ask Him to forgive me. He, our Holy God, is who I am compared to, not the neighbor next door, or child molester in prison. I am not worthy and fall short. All the good things I try to do to make myself worthy and valuable, are empty next to God. I ask the One who paid the price for me, the One who loves me perfectly, to save me. I give myself, the only sacrifice I have to give, to God in exchange for this forgiveness. Once we have established this foundation of our faith, we walk it out. Next it is time to forgive ourselves and others.

Awareness is the first step to the healing that forgiveness brings. Like Dr. Phil says, "You can't change what you don't own." This forgiveness journey is a process of awareness and receiving.

As we become aware of our inner-critic and the things we feel guilty about, we ask God to help us to forgive ourselves. Satan uses the words spoken to us after we have been betrayed to condemn us within our hearts. God will begin to show us how words of inner blame cause us to attack, revile, and even hate ourselves. We ask God to forgive us for being so unkind to our own selves. Saying out loud those words to myself, *"Chris, I forgive you for making the mistake of trusting your dad. Kids are supposed to trust their dads. Dads are supposed to be safe and what happened is not your fault,"* changed everything. It caused a breakthrough of self-rejection and condemnation and enabled me to begin to heal.

After we forgive ourselves, we ask God to forgive us for being so hard on ourselves. Just like a human dad gets upset when his kids are picked on and bullied, so does God. Even if it is us bullying ourselves. So, we say, "Please forgive me for being so mean to myself. Teach me to love me."

Next, we forgive others. Not an easy thing. Please let me be clear here...forgiving others *does not* require a relationship with them. God is completely safe and does not want us to be harmed or abused. We can forgive others and heal our hearts of the resentment and hatred we have towards them, yet still keep them out of our lives.

Forgiveness has two strands. Asking those we have hurt to forgive us and forgiving those who have hurt us. When possible, we go to those we have hurt, lied to, betrayed, stolen from, or sinned against, and tell them we are sorry and ask to be forgiven. Then we ask God to forgive us. Lastly, we forgive ourselves.

When we feel guilty and are reminded of our failures, we go through this three-step process, forgiveness with God, with others, and with ourselves.

Unfortunately, Satan will continue to attack us. He will try to get us to feel guilty so that we live in the regret of our past. Every so often, a little video or tape recording will be played in our brains after we have completed the forgiveness process. This guilt is not from God. In cases such as these, God tells us to take captive our thoughts. This means we are self-aware of what the enemy is trying to do...make us feel guilty and ashamed. We do not allow him to do this.

We demolish arguments and every pretension that sets itself up against the knowledge of God, and we take captive every thought to make it obedient to Christ.

—1 Corinthians 10:5 NIV

God says that our sins are removed from us, "as far as the east is from the west." Mathematically this can be drawn as a ↔. The point of each side of the ray will go on forever and never cross nor meet again. Our sins are infinitely removed from us never to return.

So, since our sin has been removed and we have been forgiven, being reminded of past mistakes to make us feel guilty and ashamed, is the work of the enemy. Living in guilt is not from God. Just like we do not harp on something our children did that is over and done with, nor does God. In circumstances like this we take captive the guilty thought. We are like investigators, "Ah ha! That thought is a lie!" We reframe the lie with the truth. It looks something like this:

"No, I am no longer guilty for having that affair. I forgive him. I pray his wife would forgive me and I bless her. I forgive myself, and God forgives me. Guilty thoughts leave me in the name of Jesus."

"No, I no longer feel shame about that abortion. God forgives me and I forgive myself. Guilt leave me in the name of Jesus."

"No, I no longer feel ashamed and hatred for myself because I had sex for money. God forgives me, I forgive myself, and I, by God's grace and power even choose to forgive the men who used me."

With practice, this becomes as simple as turning our attention away from the lie and praying quickly in the name of Jesus. It will become instinctual and we will soon live free from feelings of guilt.

Forgiveness for some of our hurt and betrayal is so monumental that it is impossible to do with our own power. This was the case regarding my sexual abuse. For this type of sin, we can remind God that He is "In" us. We can tell Him that we are powerless to forgive on our own, but we want to forgive. It is our *will* to forgive.

> *"Father, I want to forgive my dad, but I can't. I am still bitter, angry, and hurt. But you told me to forgive, so I am choosing to forgive. Jesus you are in me. Come by your mercy, power, and grace and enable me to forgive. I choose forgiveness and I bless my dad. I trust that soon I will be able to 'feel' like I have forgiven him."*

I wasn't sure it would happen, but by using the above process, I have forgiven those who hurt me the most. Amazingly, I feel no more bitterness or anger. You will be able to do this too if you sincerely give your heart to God in this process.

Awakening our Hearts

One of the big consequences of shame is that we may not know our own hearts. Of course, all of us have the same basic desires. We want our physical needs to be met, then our relational and financial needs as well. We desire love, enough money, and a nice safe home full of peace and happiness. These desires are legitimate, appropriate, and good. Acknowledging these desires and receiving from God is part of our restoration process.

Some of these desires being fulfilled are easy to recognize and doing so makes us feel grateful. For example, I grew up poor and often dreamed about having a swimming pool in my backyard. *"What would it be like to wake up and be able to swim anytime you wanted?"* I would think. Now, every time I back-float in my pool, I am amazed and grateful that God fulfilled this dream.

Many of our heart's desires are being fulfilled now in our lives, but there is still more to this. Could there be specific, unique, preferences and desires we have lost touch with because of shame? I believe the answer is yes.

Having wrestled with this for many years, I can testify that shame and dysfunction interfere with us receiving and even knowing our heart's desire. Because of shame, we may have detached ourselves from what we want. I remember a season of being so sad when I read the scripture

> *Take delight in the Lord, and He will give you the desires of your heart.*
>
> —Psalm 37:4 NIV

I had no idea what my desire was other than to make everyone else happy. This was a big promise from God and all I could do was ask others, "What do you want? Whatever you want is what I want. What makes you happy, makes me happy." I could not tell you what I wanted, preferred, or desired; other than whatever would please those around me. I was detached from owning my wants and not able to articulate my needs.

My friend shared that she was struggling with articulating her wants. We talked about how she might be able to practice simple ways of owning her desires. Here is an example of what we talked about:

Whenever she went out to pizza with her large family, she would seat herself last, usually at the end of the table where all the needy, little ones were seated. She would eat whatever kind of pizza everyone else wanted. We talked about what it might look like if occasionally she sat in the middle of the table, amongst the other adults. I asked her what kind of pizza she liked. She said, "I don't care." I asked her, "If you were eating by yourself and money was no object, what kind of pizza would you order?" She told me it would be, "Pepperoni, bacon, and jalapeno." I said, "Could you sit in the middle with the adults and say what you prefer?" How would it feel to say, "I don't care what kind you get, but make sure there is a half that has pepperoni, bacon, and jalapeno this time for me?"

We both were stunned at how simple this was, and yet it did not feel natural. Disregarding our preferences felt natural. Is it okay for us to state our preferences?

As we are allowing our hearts to awaken to wants and desires, we can practice articulating them in small ways like the example above. Why does it feel so uncomfortable to say what we want and need? It has to do with *vulnerability*.

First, to understand the importance of vulnerability, watch Brene Brown's, *The Power of Vulnerability* on You Tube. (TED, 2011) It's about 20 minutes long… here's the link: https://youtu.be/iCvmsMzlF7o.

We are not able to live as the authentic, "real us" unless we are willing to be vulnerable.

Neediness and speaking up about our wants and needs feels too vulnerable. First, we need to ask if we are okay with being needy.

Neediness is part of our humanity. We all have needs. Many of us are only comfortable being the "need meeter" for others. We are perfectly willing to step in and help those who are hurting, lonely, and struggling; but we are not comfortable expressing our own needs. When this happens, we are only offering others a one-dimensional relationship. When we squelch our neediness altogether, we are hiding. If we want vulnerability, and consequently real relationships, we must allow our neediness to surface.

Forming real relationships and embracing vulnerability is a process. There are three factors for consideration regarding vulnerability. One, not everyone is worthy of being trusted with our hearts when we are vulnerable. Two, we get to decide if, when, and with whom we choose to be vulnerable. And three, there are ways to be real, vulnerable, and transparent, and not give much care to whether someone "gets us," "likes us," or "approves of us."

The word vulnerable means capable of being physically or emotionally wounded, Open to an attack. Brene Brown's definition is uncertainty, risk, and emotional exposure.

That feeling of dread, the "should I or shouldn't I speak up about this?" indicates that we care about the answer to our needs. For many of us, we would rather be silent about our needs, than to reveal them and be rejected or ignored. It hurts more to tell your husband, "I need you to make love with me," and have him not respond positively, than to not mention that you miss the love making at all. It hurts more to say, "Hey, I miss hanging out. I miss our friendship," and not have our friend reciprocate, rather than to not speak up about the friendship at all.

When we speak up about something that matters to us from our hearts, it feels dangerous, because the person we are sharing with may reject us and our need. So, we don't speak up, or we deny our neediness all together. The trouble with not speaking up is that we lose the chance of a positive response. Being silent *guarantees,* we miss out. We miss some passionate love making or getting our friend back. Yes, we avoid the bad, but we miss the good as well.

Vulnerability is essential to the formation of close intimate relationships. When we refuse to expose ourselves by stating our wants, desires and needs, we lose out on the close connections to the deepest places of our hearts. We miss out on getting our heart's desires.

You see, there is power in openness and vulnerability that facilitates close relational connection. I call it, "Being the naked one in the room." When someone is willing to be transparent and real, "to be naked" and share their heart and needs, or to share past pains and shame; it breaks down the walls that others have built around them. Not only does it cause us to connect deeply to our own hearts, but "exposing" this part of us enables others to risk and be vulnerable as well. And this is how close relational connections happen.

Being Vulnerable and Safe at the Same Time

Dysfunction and some of our family belief grids have caused us some confusion regarding vulnerability. We have developed necessary ways of protecting ourselves because of the family and friendship dynamics we were raised in. These patterns were good and appropriate at the time because we lacked power when we were younger. They helped us to cope with our situations. But we are not children and we now have tools to decide if, and when, we want to be vulnerable.

1. We never "have" to be vulnerable, to share our hearts, needs, pain or shame with anyone ever. We get to choose.

2. We can choose to not share our heart's pain with those who have demonstrated that they are not safe. However, we can still tell them what we want and what we desire.

3. We have a small inner voice we listen to called the Holy Spirit. It will tell us when to speak and when to be silent. We can learn to trust that voice.

Now, we get to decide if our vulnerability could open the door for someone else to share their hearts. This is one of the ways God will work "good" from our stories of pain, by helping others who have a similar past. The hard part here is that vulnerability *ALWAYS* includes risk. Stating your preference, wants and desires, does not guarantee you will get what you wanted or asked for. You can ask for that pizza to include "pepperoni, bacon, and jalapeno," but when the pizza arrives, your request might have been ignored.

There is always the risk of disappointment when we share our needs and they are not met. How can we avoid the pain in those circumstances? The truth is we cannot avoid the pain, but we can diminish it.

Notice the word choice in the above sentence...diminish. We can reduce the pain of rejection, scorn, and even betrayal, but there is no such thing as an emotionally pain-free life.

Tool # 2 - *Giving up our Rights* is useful in these situations. Because we love ourselves and want deeper relationships with others, we can say what we want, need, and feel. These stated wants, needs and feelings *WILL NOT* always be accepted, understood, or confirmed. When the hurt begins to bubble up, we say, "I give up my right to be understood. I give up my right to be accepted. I give up my right to have this need met. Jesus was not always understood, nor accepted; so, I won't be either." Giving up our rights diminishes our hurt.

The good news, in fact, the great news regarding "need meeting," is that the Bible promises that God will meet our every need.

> *And my God will meet all your needs according to the riches of his glory in Christ Jesus.*
> —Philippians 4:19 NIV

Having needs that humans cannot meet is one of the ways we connect to God. God will not only meet our spiritual and material needs, but He will meet our relational needs as well. When we are not perfectly loved or understood, we can be grateful that there is someone who sees and understands us. God often allows unmet needs to be the very thing that draws us into deeper understanding of Him, His love, and His power.

The most powerful way to grow in being more authentic and vulnerable is to learn what God says about us. We can receive what God says about us into our hearts. We choose to agree with Him about what He says we are. We are His chosen, beloved children. It pleases God when we come to agree with Him regarding our loveliness. He formed us. This means, that my beautiful aging face is selected and formed by Him. He gave me my personality and quirks, He chose me. God chose you. God loves us! Therefore, we should love ourselves. We are worthy; worthy of His love; worthy of loving ourselves. And we are worthy of receiving love from others.

All of humanity seeks answers to: "Why do I matter?" "How can I prove to the world that I matter?" "Am I worthy of connection?"

"How can I prove I am worthy?" "Am I seen? Am I noticed? Does anyone care?" God is the God who sees. He says that we matter. When we live grounded in the foundational facts of God's love for us, we can live "real."

> *"Real isn't how you are made," said the Skin Horse. "It's a thing that happens to you. When a child loves you for a long, long time not just to play with, but REALLY loves you, then you become Real."*
> —*The Velveteen Rabbit* by Margery Williams

This is a quote from my all-time favorite Children's book, *The Velveteen Rabbit*. When we are loved for a long, long time, not just to play with, but when we are really loved, we become real, authentic, and whole. The "us," who the enemy tried to squelch, shut down and chase into hiding, can be seen. We glorify God as we live out of who He says we are.

Because the greatest authority in the Universe says I am loved, worthy, and valuable, I can release all of those lies I was taught by the lower authorities in my life. Because we are loved…

1. We choose. We decide how vested we are in a relationship. We are not required to be vulnerable with everyone.

2. We desire true intimacy with others, so when we choose to be vulnerable and authentic, we understand there may be a cost. Others hearing our truth may make them have to face some uncomfortable truths themselves.

3. We recognized that as we embrace greater authenticity and vulnerability, our family systems may balk. The way we have

functioned in our relationships has *worked for them*. Therefore, they may not appreciate our new transparency.

4. We communicate our true thoughts, feelings, and desires from a position of safety. We can do this because we are completely loved and accepted by God. Thus, we don't take ownership or responsibility for how others respond.

Review of Tools:

Review last week's tools: *Reframing*. Were you able to use it? Was it helpful? Share if you were able to use any of previously learned tools.

Tool # 12 - Making Friends with Yourself; a Process

Many of us know ourselves well enough to describe ourselves as having "parts." There may be a public self or persona you put on, and then a private reserved self. There may be a creative leader within you as well as a reluctant hider who is afraid to take the lead. There may be a part of you that wants to fit the worldly ideal of physical beauty, and a part of you that just wants to be loved for who and how they are. It is time to make friends with every part of yourself.

This tool is an ongoing process. Whenever we realize that we feel inwardly conflicted, like there are two sides of ourselves, we can make friends with both those sides of us. Both sides constitute the "real us." We may have allowed, or chosen one side to dominate because of fear, or lack of self-confidence. We may compartmentalize and not allow all the facets of us to be present in every situation. These were appropriate coping strategies when we were kids. This process acknowledges our inner complexity. We embrace, and recognizes that we are lovely, complex individuals.

- In prayer or meditation, introduce your two sides to one another.
- *"Chris who isolates, meet Chris the star of the show. Ordinary Chris, meet extraordinary Chris!"* Imagine them meeting, hugging, and loving one another.
- You may see the two sides of yourself merge into one "you."
- Imagine your heart opening like a flower as it blossoms. Allow both sides to feel the deep love and compassion you have for yourself.

Tool # 13 - Inner Healing Prayer

Inner healing prayer is when you ask the Holy Spirit to show you "why" you feel, believe, react, or function in a particular way. It is a very deep and powerful tool used in Christian counseling. It is used to get to the root of the "why" behind behavior and beliefs. The "whys" behind our, behavior, feelings, words, reactions, and beliefs are sometimes based upon the big life events of our past.

*Please refer to the Tool appendix in the back of the book for details on this process.

Questions for Discussion

1. How good are you at accepting yourself as you are...not the improved, idealized version? Not the thinner, fitter, funnier, cuter version of you?

2. How good are you at saying what you want?

3. What makes you jealous or envious? This can give us clues into what we are desiring.

4. Name a quirk about yourself that you love.

5. Are you able to communicate a full range of emotion in the appropriate situation?

6. Name a time you needed help but did not ask for it.

7. Do you agree with the statement that you most fully Glorify God when you are authentic?

ART CONNECTION

God's Glory and Your Glory

Materials:

String or yarn
8.5 by 11-inch sheet of paper (per person)
One poster board or large sheet of butcher paper
Markers, pens, colored pencils, or *colored pastel chalks* (Preferred)
Hair spray to set the pastel chalk (if needed)

Method: On page 148 is a list of positive attributes. Use the list to create a picture of "God's Glory" and his relationship to you and the unique gifts and talents He created within you. See the sample on the next page for clarity.

- Using the poster board or large sheet of butcher paper, draw a picture to represent "God's Glory." The picture should have swirls of color and be round like the sun. Brainstorm/Write some of the attributes of God on the picture. Then write each person's name around the edge of the circle, going outward from the center of "God." (This represents that each person is a part of God displaying His glory to the world.)
- Then, each individual will use an 8.5 x 11-inch paper to create another swirl of colors that represent you and your glory. Brainstorm/Write some of your good traits/attributes around the edges of your circle.
- Use the positive attribute list on the following page to list the

gifts, talents, and abilities that God has given you. List as many as you can think of.

- When everyone is finished coloring and listing their positive attributes, share your abilities with the group. If you are not able to come up with much, leave some blank spaces. Other people may have to tell you the gifts and talents they see in you. (This may indicate you need healing. Is it perfection? Are you hard on yourself? Does not acknowledging the gifts God gave you glorify God?)
- Next, lay the pictures in a circle alongside the larger "God's Glory" picture. Use the string to indicate arrows of connections we have to God and His Glory as we are connected with God and His glory.
- This project makes a great display. It will have the large picture of God's Glory in the center and all the smaller pictures encircling it. If you have a dedicated space, you might want to hang it on the wall.

Take pictures with your cameras of all the pictures surrounding the God's Glory picture. Share your results with one another. Ask questions and pray.

God's Glory Sample Art

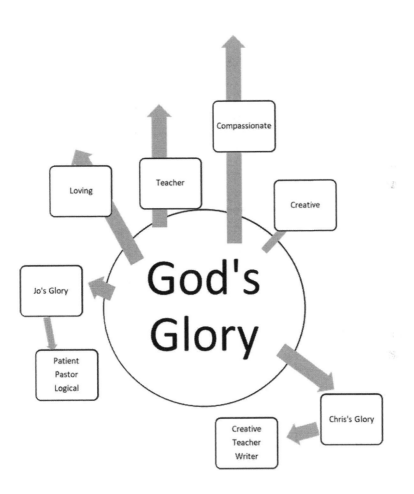

Positive Attribute Traits

Accountable	Adaptable	Adventurous
Assertive	Astute	Attentive
Authentic	Brave	Capable
Calm	Committed	Communicator
Compassionate	Considerate	Consistent
Creative	Dedicated	Determined
Discerning	Disciplined	Easy-going
Energetic	Enthusiastic	Expressive
Fair	Faithful	Fearless
Friendly	Generous	Grateful
Happy	Hard-working	Honest
Humorous	Imaginative	Integrity
Intelligent	Joyful	Knowledgeable
Listener	Loving	Loyal
Nurturing	Open-minded	Optimistic
Organized	Patient	Peaceful
Practical	Punctual	Resourceful
Responsible	Reliable	Serves Others
Spiritual	Stable	Strong
Spontaneous	Tactful	Successful
Trustworthy	Truthful	Willing

CHAPTER 9

Faith Matters

The Gospel

What to Expect:

THIS CHAPTER IS KEY to the formation of healthy family systems because The Gospel answers the biggest, loudest heart cry of each individual family member: "Why do I matter?" Our worthiness and why we are worthy is The Gospel. All unhealthy family systems view love, esteem, value and worth as something outside of the system, something to be attained. The Gospel knocks all that pressure and effort to its knees. It is where we come to understand that our value, worthiness, and esteem is something that we receive from God. It reverses the paradigm from earning to receiving.

Christianity is the only religion that eliminates the great balance scale in the sky.

Objectives:

In this lesson we will explore the following:

- We are not able to earn anything from God.
- There is a difference between righteousness in the Old Testament and righteousness in the New Testament.
- Not everything in the Old Testament is applicable to the New Covenant.
- Salvation is a spiritual birth that allows Christ to dwell *IN* us.
- Walking in the flesh causes dysfunction in family systems.

The New verses Old

This might be simplistic to most Christians out there, but I would be remiss if I did not attempt to communicate the Good News. One cannot assume that just because someone professes faith in Christ, or even if they have been a Christian for years, that there is firm understanding as to what exactly happened at the Cross.

If one is asked, "What is going to happen to you when you die?" How one responds demonstrates whether an understanding of Salvation is truly grasped. If anyone replies in any way, shape, or form that it is because they are a good person, or they follow the Ten Commandments, or they attend Church, they don't understand The Gospel and are therefore watering down the gift of salvation.

Let me back up. I did not come to understand this until I had been a Christian for 25 years. I was very confused and here is why. I read the Bible as though it were all one book written to me.

The Bible is divided into two sections, The Old Testament, and the New Testament. The Old Testament was written before the birth of Jesus. It was a book written to the Jews. Even the Quran embraces the teachings of the first few books of the Old Testament because their religion is an offshoot from the lineage of Abraham.

All three religions, Jewish, Muslim, and Christian use parts of the Old Testament as an element of their sacred teachings. The Old Testament depicts what righteousness from a Holy God's perspective looks like. The New Testament was written after Jesus' birth, death, and resurrection and depicts a new "better covenant," the covenant of Grace.

For if there had been nothing wrong with that first covenant,
no place would have been sought for another.
But God found fault with the people and said:
"The days are coming, declares the Lord,
when I will make a new covenant with the people of Israel
and with the people of Judah.
It will not be like the covenant I made with their ancestors
when I took them by the hand to lead them out of Egypt,
because they did not remain faithful to my covenant,
and I turned away from them, declares the Lord.
This is the covenant I will establish
with the people of Israel after that time, declares the Lord.
I will put my laws in their minds and write them on their hearts.
I will be their God, and they will be my people.
No longer will they teach their neighbor,
or say to one another, 'Know the Lord,'
because they will all know me,
from the least of them to the greatest.
For I will forgive their wickedness
and will remember their sins no more."

By calling this covenant "new," He has made the first one obsolete;
and what is obsolete and outdated will soon disappear.
—Hebrews 8:8-13 NIV

When I studied the teachings of Jesus in the New Testament, and the meaning of Biblical grace, I discovered that Jesus did not focus on sin, instead He always provoked those who He was speaking to, to go deeper. His focus went to the heart of the issue of sin. What is the thing that you love or need that you are searching for with this sin? It was not so much the sin itself but the motivation behind a person's sin which was spotlighted. His focus was on love, and bringing us to His perfect Father, the Father of Love.

When Jesus was critical, his criticism was not directed toward the common people of His day, but rather toward the Pharisees, the religious leaders who were thought to have their act together. These would be the so-called "Super Christians" of their time. He would basically take their hundreds of laws, which the Pharisees, the devout leaders, felt that they themselves had fulfilled, and He would raise the bar higher. The Pharisees were about following the letter of the law, but often not the heart of the law.

We all pretty much can agree what sin is; stuff we do that is wrong. We could give a ten-year-old a "sin quiz" and they would pretty much be able to classify sin as the following: Lying? "Yep." Stealing? "Yep." Backstabbing? "Yep." Being mean? "Yep."

As far as I know, every religion is based on the "good" versus "evil" paradigm. Basically, it is, I do good things, I try to be a good person, I obey the law and I avoid evil; thus, I am owed:

1. God's favor and rewards.

2. Whatever eternal rewards exist in the hereafter.

3. Forgiveness and eternal life.

When I truly began to understand Grace and what Jesus accomplished on the cross, it blew away all my confusion about other religions. Christianity is not based on good works. In fact, working your way into Heaven is detestable to God. It is the only religion that eliminates the great balance scale in the sky.

What I discovered about Grace is, not only does God want you to avoid sin, but performing to erase your shame, performing to earn your way to heaven, or to earn his favor, is not his desire. Instead, He wants us to simply *receive* His Righteousness. My previous error, and it was a doozy, was looking at God through the eyes of the Old Testament.

I did not believe it at first when my friend taught me there was a division between the Old and New Testament. Sacrilege! She said I was combining all the scriptures together as though they were all written to me. After all, they are all bound in the same book, right?

It took a while to decide whether to believe that there was a difference between the two and it just wasn't all "in the Bible" with equal weight and meaning. I finally concluded that yes, there is a difference.

Just from a historical perspective, the New Testament was not even written until after Jesus' resurrection. Christianity began without any scriptures, just the stories of Jesus passed down from witnesses. They document his life as well as how the Holy Spirit moved and directed the steps of believers to form the early Church.

The New Testament is a compilation of various authors. There were separate manuscripts which were written independently of one another, but which all validated the stories and words of Jesus. Separate accounts but cohesive in the telling. These accounts, recorded by eyewitnesses during his time on earth, have been interpreted from their original languages and complied into the book we call the New Testament. They were written in the decades after Jesus' death and resurrection.

Later, religious leaders decided to combine the two, calling it the Old and New, and placing it all together in the Bible as one book. No wonder I was confused.

Old Testament = Judgment New Testament = Grace

The Old Testament was the book for the Jews. The Old Testament was about religious laws, and what constitutes goodness and holiness from the eyes of a perfect God. The New Testament is about Jesus, the Savior of the world, who *provides* the perfection and holiness required by a perfect God *in our stead*. He brings us close to the Father through *faith* in Him and nothing else.

The Old Testament had 613 laws. Much of it is full of wisdom that is practiced even today, such as crop rotation and allowing the soil to rest every seven years. There were sanitary commands, practices that have since been proved to be beneficial by science. These 613 laws range from commands on "big sins," like thou shall not kill, and thou shall not commit adultery, to obscure laws, like not eating dairy and meat at the same time, (adios cheeseburgers), and not sacrificing an animal with damaged testicles. Jesus fulfilled all 613 laws.

When He would preach, often speaking to the Pharisees about the law, He always did so in a way that would confront their hypocrisy. He was basically saying, "You hold yourself up as an example as one who is holy, who pleases God," and then He would up the ante. Matthew 5: 17-48 illustrates this as Jesus teaches (Paraphrased):

> *"You say you don't murder. If you even think about hurting someone when you are* angry *with your brother, you are guilty. You think you don't commit adultery, but if you even look at a woman in a lustful way, you have committed adultery in your heart."*

Because the Old Testament was written before the ushering in of Grace, at Jesus' ascension, many of the stories are lessons about judgment and the consequences of sin.

Before I came to really understand the Bible and the difference between The Law of the Old Testament and The Grace of the New Testament, I was often afraid of God. I had no discernment and was often terrified as I read the Old Testament. Many of the teachings from the Old Testament were like hooks that would catch my guilty heart. I felt so defective, like all those "Woe to you," verses were meant for me. I knew that the Old Covenant required obedience to please God, and I was always failing to obey. I would identify with the sinful characters and become afraid that I would receive the same consequences they received - especially since I had the same behavior. Yikes!

I had two major issues that caused me to misunderstand Salvation. One, I did not understand the new birth and what it meant for God's Spirit to come into us. And two, I did not understand what the Bible means when it speaks of "walking in the Flesh."

At Salvation, I was given a new heart and nature. Jesus came to live *IN* me.

Before He was born, crucified, and resurrected, no one had God living inside of them. The Holy Spirit might have led prophets or priests, but did not reside *IN* them. Now, at salvation, Christ stays in us forever.

One of the most confusing things for me regarding the Spirit and my new heart was the word righteousness. In the Old Testament righteousness is the form of *doing* right. If you do everything "right" God will be pleased with you. It is mostly embodied by following all 613 just and moral laws set forth by God, an impossibility of course. That is why it foreshadows a Savior, a Messiah, who will deliver us.

In the New Testament, righteousness has a different form. It means the *quality of being* morally right or justified, free from the guilt of sin. The first form is an action, things we humans should do to be holy. While the second form *is a state of being, an impartation* that happens at Salvation.

I no longer do right to "become right" with God. I am operating under this new form of righteousness, which is Christ is *IN* me. I am *IN* Him. I am new. I have a new heart. I am no longer spiritually dead in my sins because God's Spirit is *IN* me. I am now *RIGHT*. My righteousness is not something I have to do to earn God's favor, love, or earn my way to heaven. It is something I receive and stand in.

God sees me as right, not wrong. I am good. I am holy. I am a saint. I am free. I have a new heart and a new nature. My new nature does not want to sin. When I make choices that conflict with this new nature, life does not go well for me. I am free to choose anything I want, even to sin, and God will still, and does still, have the same love for me.

I know many of you are reading this and going, "Woah, woah, whoa… stop right there Missy. What about sin?" you may ask. "Are you saying God is okay with Sin?" And this leads to the second part of The Gospel I did not grasp. As believers in Christ, we no longer have a sin problem. We have a flesh problem. Many of us do not grasp this concept of scripture.

The reason why we still see sinful behavior in believers is because we often choose to walk in the flesh. We have been given freedom to choose. We either choose to walk by the Spirit or to walk by the flesh. And this gets to the crux of the problem for those Christian families that are dealing with dysfunction. We have the freedom of choice. We can choose rage, control, manipulation, discord, or selfishness; or we can choose to love. Walking in the flesh can be very satisfying in the moment. Lashing out when we are angry, loudly defending our side when we experience an injustice, controlling others so that we can get our way, all meet a surface desire. But flesh begets flesh. Rage in us incites rage in others. Selfishness brings about "every man for himself" in others. Walking by the Spirit sows love. The truth is that when we are walking in the fullness of love, we will not sin.

Think about those times you are fully aware and experiencing the Love of God. When we are in this state, we are gentle, kind, hopeful, and have self-control. When we walk in the Spirit, we want what God wants, and we are empowered to carry it out.

As we look at the Gospel from the perspective of healing our hearts so that we can heal our families, it comes down to love. Receiving God's love. We first understand God's unconditional love for us. God sees us as worthy and valuable, His perfect little child. This is some good news. Our salvation was a spiritual birth that cannot be undone. God, our Father, will always see us through the eyes of the perfection of Jesus. The love and graciousness of this truth changes us. Our response is worship, thanksgiving, and awe.

Now we are equipped to learn about the healthy love God wants us to teach our families. First, we change. Then, God will enable us to walk by the Spirit so that we can choose the highest good for our families. Walking by the Spirit will cause us to become safer people. As we receive the understanding of Salvation, our actions, words, choices, and behaviors will change to become more Christ-like. We will choose to love others, not necessarily please everyone, but to love others. We will walk in the Spirit and heal our families.

Review of Tools:

Review last week's tools: *Making Friends with Yourself* and *Inner Healing Prayer*. Were you able to use them? Were they helpful? Share if you were able to use any of previously learned tools.

An Invitation to Faith

You are cordially invited
To

Become A Child of The Most-
High God.
You will become Holy.
Come receive love.
Be made righteous.

Just

Pray and ask Jesus to be your Savior.
Ask Him to come into your heart.
Tell Him you are sorry for your past.

Be made NEW.

RSVP: NOW

ASK God to flood you with His
Holy Spirit.

Questions for Discussion

1. Do you believe that God sees you as righteous?

2. Have you ever been confused about the Old Testament and the New Testament?

3. Have you prayed to ask Christ into your heart? If not, what holds you back? Talk about that.

4. What do you think it means, *"Christianity is the only religion that takes away the great balance scale in the sky?"*

5. What was something that you misunderstood from the Bible in the past, but have clarity on now?

ART CONNECTION

The Doorway of Intimacy

Materials:

8.5 by 11-inch paper
Pencils, Markers, and Crayons

Method: In this art project you will be provided an opportunity to assess your intimacy with Jesus. Remember, we are all growing in intimacy with God if we have asked Him into our heart. Just like marriage, we may have seasons of closeness and then feel disconnected. This is a similar phenomenon to our faith walk. Just like in our intimate relationships, we can choose to reconnect.

Using paper and markers draw a door. Then draw a room. Jesus says that He stands at the door and knocks. This symbolizes Him asking to be let into our hearts.

- Where you are in the fellowship of intimacy with Jesus?
- Have you welcomed Him in through the door?
- How far has Jesus crossed the threshold into the room?
- Are you in the room together? What kind of a room is it?
- How do you interact with one another?
- Is the door open, but one of you is outside of the room?
- Is there something that you fear letting go of that hinders your intimacy with God?
- Have you been disconnected? Why is that?

Pray first until an image in formed in your mind. Once you feel led, draw the door and how you view yourself in intimacy with God. Do you want more connection? Does God want more connection with you? Once you sit in silence and an image comes to you, you may begin.

Share your picture, ask questions, and then pray for one another.

If you are not a believer, sit in silence until an image comes to you. Share it with one another and ask questions.

CHAPTER 10

Shame Matters

The Church and Shame

What to Expect:

THIS CHAPTER IS WRITTEN because The Church is called to love others. Love is exponential and The Church is where God has chosen to demonstrate the power of this multiplicity. When we love, we invest something supernaturally into another person which enables them to love more and love better. For example: If a population of Christ-followers doubled their "love" connection with one person every month, we would have two, then four, then eight, 16, 32, 64, 128, 256, and so on. Shame blocks us from receiving love. It blocks connection and therefore it blocks God and the Holy Spirit. So, the chapter ahead discusses shame and its effects on The Church. It also confronts the fact that shame causes us to love as a theory rather than an action.

Objectives:

In this lesson we will explore the following:

- People carry shame with them.

- Many people are reluctant to go to church because of shame.
- Many Christians feel like "Church people don't 'get' them" because of shame.
- The Church will not be able to fully meet the needs of people unless we are willing to address the issue of shame.
- Each of us have "people" that God has appointed us to befriend.

Caring for the Hurting

This section is to my beloved sisters and brothers of faith. I have always loved churches and have visited so many different denominations. One of the good things about having parents who never take you to church, is that there is no allegiance to a particular denomination. I am grateful to God's people, and the variety of ways we worship God. Most of us came to know Jesus while attending or visiting one of the traditional churches in America. Certainly, our faith grew in connection with others in church settings. I am grateful for the heritage of faith that our country was founded upon.

The traditional church in America has been, and is, a powerful force of God. When we, the people of God, tune into what He is saying, the Holy Spirit may move us in a new direction. The Church in America witnessed this in the last 15 years. Worship changed. In almost every denomination, many believers, especially younger believers, were no longer satisfied with traditional worship. Worship became a pathway to deeper intimacy with God. This pleased God. He placed the desire within us to express our love for Him openly in song with many arms lifted high.

I am writing this chapter while knowing ahead of time, that not every believer is going to like it, or agree with it. I believe God wants to move The Church in a new direction. He wants The Church to understand the deep heart needs of wounded people and to equip us with tools to heal the hurting. To begin this change, The Church needs to understand shame.

It is my belief that many of my Christian brothers and sisters do not understand shame and the way it affects both believers as well as non-believers. Dealing with shame also affects how the world views The Church. You see, some of my biggest hurt happened in church. Let me explain the dynamics of shame and how it affects those who might be trying out "church."

Shame caused me to have two selves. There was the public one who was together, smart, articulate, wearing her makeup, and always trying to be perfect. But there was also my ordinary self, the "nothing special about her" girl. She was afraid to go to parties. It always took effort and energy to interact in public. She could psyche the other Chris, the together one, to go in her place. She longed for close friendship, but did not easily allow others in. Experience had taught her that people were not to be trusted. Too many times she was the sucker, falling into unsafe relationships time and again.

However, hope would arise. Could this be THE group? Could this be THE time when it will finally happen? Will I connect closely with other Christians? After all, this IS a Bible study!

Make up on, wearing something cute, but not too sexy, she would set out to make friends, to make the deep connections she longed for... only to be hurt. She would open up, hinting of past abuse, only to find no one willing to go "there." She always felt exposed, the only naked one in the room. Oh, they would always "be in prayer" for her...boy would they pray for her. However, she always felt emotionally bare...vulnerable. She believed she didn't fit in anywhere, even at church. "Why don't church people get me," she would wonder?

There are many of us who feel that church isn't for those with real problems and struggles. There are many who have been disconnected to a body of fellowship because of hurt in churches. It seems like church is the place you go once you have your life figured out. Many believe that we should keep the stink of a messy life at home. Church is where we put our best relational foot forward, not crossing the threshold if we don't have our collective "stuff" together. Are there hurting "messes" out there? You bet!

In my view, The Church up to 2019[1] has focused on messages that are out of balance for those who struggle with shame. We, The Church, have good intentions. We know our God is one of power. We know He provides this power for us, His children. But there is a push to use scripture to try to make everyone "okay" on the surface. We understand all the promises of scripture in our head, but don't always receive it in our heart. These messages seem to about how we can use God's power and strength to achieve "togetherness." Believers who share how "together" they are, do not help those of us who carry shame.

Stories of how good life is now that you have Christ is not helpful nor healing unless you also share how bad your times of darkness were without Him. Of course we want to brag on our God. We tell about our good days, all for God's glory. We are willing to discuss

---

1. I say this because I believe that during the COVID pandemic of 2020, something is happening in the hearts of believers that is changing church as we know it.

our mountain-top experiences and our victories. However, we are not as willing to allow Him to use our very worst days for His glory.

The epidemic of shame ridden people in America, those who have addictions and histories of abuse, do not connect with the one-sided messages of The Church. We feel like we are defective and outsiders. We can't imagine our healing and it feels as if we don't belong in the traditional church.

The trouble is that there is little transparency and little vulnerability among church folk. The Church seems to communicate on the surface level. We are comforted with scripture that appeals to our mind; that we are free from shame and rejection. This is true because we are *IN* Christ, and we are free from shame and rejection. However, shame is a heart issue not just a mind issue.

It is at this point that the church is failing to facilitate healing from shame we so desperately need. This is why so many feel that "Church people don't get me." It is like we try to attain the promises of scripture in our head, but they don't stick.

I shared my belief that "Church people don't get me," with the women I minister to. Hands down, it resonated in the heart and minds of these mostly Christian women. "They don't get me either!" is the cumulative cry. Why is that? Is this issue a church issue? Or is it a, me, and my shame issue? I think it is both.

Under the "me and my shame" part lies an inability to identify who is safe and who is not safe. When wounded folks try out a church, that single act alone is one of vulnerability. Entering a building full of people who know one another and share the bond of fellowship is risky. That is why many wounded folks don't go to church. It feels too dangerous.

Shame keeps non-believers from connecting with believers. Our shame always tells us to hide. Shame tells us that if we share our real selves with these "together" people, they may not understand us. We long for connections, but we don't see The Church as a valid place to be accepted and understood. Unfortunately, The Church is deemed to be "unsafe" by many people in the world.

So, this bears the question…are Christians safe people? Are you a safe person? Am I safe? We are supposed to feel safe with followers of Christ because they are supposed to be living a higher standard. There is the expectation that Christians know how to love because they abide in the love of the Father. But do we know how to love? Are we abiding in God's love? Are we different from others who have no faith?

People who struggle with shame, keep their guard up in most of their everyday relationships. When new believers, especially those who have a dysfunctional past, seek The Church for all the good it has to offer, they must let their guard down and become vulnerable. When the Church doesn't recognize this vulnerability and eventually hurts us, it's a double-whammy wound. First, our wounds are reopened, and our soul is yet again crushed. Secondly, the view of church being "safe" is betrayed, creating disillusionment with God.

It is not totally The Church's fault, because wounded and unhealed individuals carry their shame grid into every situation. It can take just a particular look, or outright inattention to trigger the feelings of rejection and shame. The Church cannot instantly eliminate each person's shame. What we can do better, is understand shame, how prevalent it is, and be educated how to help those who need healing from its devastating effects. What we can do is to be sure that we are safe. We can take steps to understand dysfunction so that we might love one another better.

The wounded and unhealed individual must do his or her part.

There is asking for and receiving of healing that needs to be done. I encourage you to explore the following questions:

- Do I feel ashamed in front of God? Why? (See Tool # 13 - Inner Healing Prayer)
- Do I feel accepted and loved by God?
- Do I love and accept myself?
- Do I avoid connecting with other believers because of shame?
- How can I heal from feelings of shame so that I can receive what others speak of when they talk about their new identity in Christ?

We, The Church, need to ask God if we are safe people? Have we asked and allowed God to work within us? Can we keep confidences, and honor and support the hurting? Are we willing to put in the *TIME* to be our brother's keeper?

I believe that God is doing something new as He is breaking the religious systems that have been the forefront of Christianity in the United States. These programs and the "business as usual" paradigm are ending. We are moving to a divergent Church that is everywhere: breweries, homes, gyms, day-care centers, community centers and outdoor parks. These churches will be relationship-centered rather than business centered. They will be places where it will be okay to be in process and experience the messiness of life as you receive God's love.

I tried to begin support groups for sexually abused women at several different churches. I offered my time and talents for free. I was willing to talk about what no one was willing to talk about…to go public for the statistical *twenty percent* of the female congregation that have sexual abuse histories. It could have been an outreach to the community for believers and unbelievers alike. Not one church took my proposal.

Oh, I was offered the ability to lead Bible Studies and do "approved" book studies, but I couldn't do a deep-dive program addressing the needs of abused women. This type of healing did not fit within the programs and the business model of the churches I asked. They seemed to be afraid of anything new or controversial. What kind of gospel are we offering if we cannot help or even talk about our most devastating needs? What is wrong with The Church? Where is the disconnect? Do we want to offer real, active love that helps others?

So, pray with me. Pray for a teachable and humble spirit to fall upon us all. Ask the hard questions. We cannot change what we do not acknowledge. We do not receive if we do not ask.

- Does the Church really want to hear about pain?
- Does the Church teach *how* to heal?
- Does the Church want to embrace to *idea* of healing the broken, or *actually* healing the broken?
- Are we willing to give *time* to those that hurt? Or will we toss out the, "I'll be praying for you" …and then share someone's sacred pain with another under the guise of prayer?
- How does The Church address the shame of believers?
- Does the Church in 2020 *want* to be relevant?

> Incest, porn, rape, addict, alcoholic, molestation, cutters,
> anxiety, bulimia,
> abortion, anorexia, depression, suicide, panic attacks,
> bi-polar disorder

Are we Christians willing to talk about the horrible abuses, mal-treatment, and illnesses in the table above? Can we break the code of silence about the darkness many are in? Can the wounded open up about these issues with all the shame and lies that accompany it? Could those who suffer find help at your church today? Is there a group for the "messed-up" and the "*NOT* okay" of us in the body of Christ? Is there anyone who has time for us? We need The Church. I wish for the sake of those who have been hurt, that it was God and God alone, working His plan on this earth. For some reason though God has chosen to use people.

Christianity is a journey of faith with two prongs, God, and people. I would not have heard about Christ if it weren't for a neighbor who saw a lost little girl and told her about Jesus. Jesus didn't come into my room and introduce Himself personally. Rather, He brought a woman who spoke and shared her faith story, then drove me to a place to learn about Christ. This pattern continues. He uses people in our stories of faith, and He uses us in the stories of others.

This "people thing" can lead to its own set of problems. Our deepest, darkest secrets involve people. Exposing our shame to the light will involve people. The journey of healing from our shame doesn't happen alone. We heal with God and with others. Interest-ingly, the most gracious forum of healing I have ever encountered has been at an Alcoholics Anonymous (AA) meeting.

AA is a group of broken, yet loving and caring people, taking a fearless moral inventory of themselves and judging none. They have committed to being trustworthy people that can carry the sanctity of each other's stories of destruction and reconstruction. I heard more about people's dirty laundry and how God was working things for their good than I have heard in all my church services.

The good news is, The Church is changing for the better. We are becoming a healed group of safe individuals. Silence is being broken and people are becoming more available and more transparent with others. We are in the midst of repentance for not caring about others.

God brought me to a deep repentance and brokenness about this myself. I thought I cared about others and thought I had a love for others. I have always wanted to help people, share The Gospel with people, and speak to groups about God. I would imagine myself before the throngs, speaking wonderful words of wisdom.

He showed me that I wanted to share God's message with people, theoretical "people," but I didn't care so much about the *person*. We can think of people as this academic, conjectural group. "People" are a theory, individuals are messy. A *person* requires involvement, interaction, and relationship. A *person* requires time, presence and caring. I was confronted with my disconnect and selfishness. This is a quote someone painted for me. It hangs on my living room wall.

> *You can't carry the light of Jesus to a world that you've made up in your mind, that is a hypothetical future, that may never happen. But you can carry the light of Jesus to the world you are walking in today.*
> —Shawn Johnson, Pastor, Red Rocks Church

With this change of heart, God brought me persons. One

particular *Art from the Heart Workshop* was six weekly meetings in a community center with just *one* person. This one person was worth the time; setting up seating, connecting technology, planning, and the sacrifice involvement takes. It was worth it to God. He was changing me so that it was worth it to me.

My hope is that we all will connect with the *persons* in our life. Showing up more, slowing down, making room to relate. Hopefully, we individuals that make up the body of Christ, will care more. I hope we become safe spaces where those who are not okay can receive love and healing. This process is messy, and we just have our little, tiny part as God directs each person's path. But we own our part. We show up for our lines, our purpose, in the divine connection with each other's God story.

So, who are your persons? Do you believe that God directs your steps? When you're talking to someone, anyone, they in that moment are your person. We need to recognize and follow through with those who come across our path. Often, we are given hints that someone needs us and we either ignore them or miss their clues.

Let me explain the dynamics of mixed messages those who hurt send out. We need to understand the bottom line needs of the people who cross our paths. We also need to recognize when we are being offered an opening to love and model Christ.

Mixed Messages of Shame

People who struggle with shame often send out two opposite messages. One is, "Come closer," and the other one is, "Stay away." It is like we are beckoning someone to come next to us with one hand, while at the same time raising the other hand up into the classic stop signal. So, neglect from the body of Christ is not necessarily a lack of caring. It can be because there are mixed messages.

Shame causes a dance of intimacy and regret. Brene Brown calls it a "Vulnerability Hangover." Our inner critic beats us up for speaking up about something that matters to our hearts, especially if it had to do with abuse or dysfunction. We might temporarily break the code of silence and tell someone honestly about a struggle, only to withdraw and beat ourselves up later. After the encounter, as we replay our every word and analyze the expressions of those we confided in, we tell ourselves that we were stupid, stupid, stupid for saying anything at all. We promise ourselves that we will never do that again.

But, deep within our hearts is a loneliness and a longing for connection. We were created for friendship and deep intimate relationships, and so, we will let ourselves be partially seen on occasion, but immediately go into hiding afterward.

Those who are willing to help the hurting, need to be aware of this dynamic. To stop the dynamic, we can say, "Wow, that was deep, and I am grateful you trusted me with this part of your heart. Let's talk and arrange to meet, but remember, the enemy is going to try to tell you how dumb you were for sharing. You are not going to listen to that voice, are you?"

In my support groups, I tell the women ahead of time, that they will hear their inner critic telling them how stupid they are for speaking. Satan hates us connecting because when the secret things done in the darkness are spoken of, they come to the light. The light heals.

Awareness of this dance and the way we regret disclosure, is the first tool of coming to the light. Understanding the pattern of disclosure and withdraw, allows us to *choose*. Being able to recognize intimacy-regret and the consequential impulse to withdraw enables us to choose better. We are able to say,

"Oh, here it is. I am beating myself up for sharing my heart and my impulse is to avoid speaking to 'John' ever again. This is the expected emotion for my situation because of my past. It is normal and I can choose to connect rather than withdraw. I choose connection."

I wish that we believers were aware of the significance of the little tidbits God gives us when we are being given an opportunity to love. When we hear, "I was abused..." "There was a lot of violence in our home..." "I was in foster care..." "I was raped..." "I had an abortion..." or "I struggle with addiction...", we are being offered hints about someone's deep pain. When we have a glimpse into someone else's story, we can learn to recognize the significance of this momentary trust and be present. God is saying in this moment, "Here is a hurting one. Will you help?" And "This is a *person* I put in your path. Can you lend an ear for a moment?"

I think many people give a platitude saying they will "be in prayer" for the hurting individual because they feel inadequate to help. I have two things to say to this. First, it does not depend on you. God is the healer. Second, God must have thought you have something to offer because you are the one, He crossed this person's path with.

We cannot heal anyone, but we can ask questions and listen. We might exchange phone numbers and tell the person that we appreciate them trusting us enough to share. We can assure them that this will go no further - and honor that. We can ask them if they would like to meet to pray together. This provides them with a chance to have a relationship and diminished loneliness. You don't have to be "qualified," just be a friend who is willing to pray with them. God is the healer and teacher; we just walk along side and love.

Review of Tools:

I have introduced and reviewed all 13 tools. Were you able to use any of them? Were they helpful? Share your experiences.

Tool # 3 - Talking to God/Prayer

As a review, Prayer is the weapon we have been given to fight the enemy. If any of this resonates within you, the place we go for healing and change is to our God.

This is a time to pray and ask God if He wants to use you in a deeper way to connect with other people. The following are some ideas of what to pray about with regard to this chapter.

- Is there something in my heart that is off limits to you God?
- Do you want to increase my ability to care about other people?
- Do I have shame myself that You want to heal?
- Am I willing to allow You to use all of my life, even the painful and shameful parts, to connect with and heal others as you lead me?

Questions for Discussion

1. Have you experienced hurt in Church?

2. Do you ever send out mixed messages of shame? What are they?

3. Who of the people has God used in your life to bring your *heart* closer to Him?

4. Are you able to share a time you felt disappointed or betrayed which caused you to not want to interact with people? It is not necessary to talk about this unless you feel comfortable. The question is, ARE you able to talk about it?

5. Have you been able to find one person that was safe enough to share this story?

6. Have you ever had an experience where it was safe to share the deep places of your heart? Was this in a church setting?

7. Talk about a time you felt God was using something that had been difficult in your life to help another person who had a similar struggle.

ART CONNECTION

Here's the Church, Here's the Steeple, Open the Door, See all the People

Materials:

8.5 by 11-inch paper
Colored markers, crayons, colored pencils

Method: This art project is designed to illustrate the unique sphere of influence, love, and faith walk, that God has ordained you to share with others.

- Using the paper and a colored marker or pencil, trace your palm. Think of your hand in the "open" position to model giving. Trace the palm in the center of the paper.
- Pray and ask the Holy Spirit to show you all your various connections to people and spheres of influence.
- Draw a shape or space off of each finger indicating a physical location that you visit, live in, or work in, on a daily or weekly basis. Label those locations.
- Then ask if there is a particular person in each location who might need a friendly ear. Is there someone who God might want you to show His love to? Label them in the space or location.
- Take time to pray and tell God that you are willing to give the gift of time if He opens the door for you to have an authentic connection with this person. Tell Him that you are willing,

but that it cannot be forced or manipulated. Ask Him who are your people. Ask Him to make you care more.

First, take time to pray. Ask the Holy Spirit where is your sphere of influence and who are your "persons." Remain in silence until an image is formed in your mind. Begin when you feel led to do so. Share with the group. Discuss and pray.

Tools

Tools You Can Use

Our greatest tool is Jesus and his abiding presence giving us the power to respond differently than we have in the past.

CONGRATULATIONS TO YOU FOR reading this far in the book! I want to encourage you because there is much happiness and joy in the process of becoming a healthier family member. You will not heal from, nor process the past all at once. There is a gentle ebb and flow in the progression of change. But you can do this! Remember, we are "perfect, being made perfect." We do things going forward with our family's "highest good" in mind.

Most of the chapters in this book provide tools to support your efforts to heal unhealthy family relationships. They are "how to" tools. Their intent is to provide active help as we learn to relate to our families in healthier ways. These tools are especially helpful in dealing with fear and anxiety. We subconsciously control others in our family systems *because we are afraid*. Our healing comes in choosing new and better ways to respond to our families. This process will cause us to address our fears, as we relinquish control and deal with the emotions that this entails. Remember, when something painful in our life occurs, God does not just leave us to struggle alone!

Each one of these tools are available if and when you need them, 24/7. Their purpose is to diminish the emotional pain which arises when we are called to change particular relationship dynamics in our families. They are powerful and enable us to be honest and let go of whether others approve of us. I hope they are helpful to you.

I feel the best way to implement these tools is to personalize them. Ask God to help adapt the following actions and prayers to meet your needs. Write them down in your journal or on index cards. Recite them and practice frequently until you feel comfortable with their use. And most importantly, keep track of the emotion or action that triggers the need for each particular tool. That way, when a tool's need arises, you are ready for action!

Tool # 1 - Giving Yourself Time

The first tool is giving yourself time to heal. We did not get where we are today in our unhealthy dynamics in a moment. We do not change in a moment either. Yes, I believe that God can heal in a moment. I prayed for years that all the painful memories of my past would be swept away instantaneously. I received prayer with the laying on of hands hoping for this type of healing, but that is not how God chose to help me. "Why not?" you may ask. "Wouldn't it be easier and quicker? Isn't that part of God, that He heals us?"

The Gospel is not about living a pain free life. It is about loving God, ourselves, and others. First and foremost, God wants us to *KNOW* Him. Coming closer to God and a resultant change of heart accompanies this process. That is why I think God does not heal our beliefs and emotions instantaneously. There is a change in us that occurs. If I would have just had my memories of the past removed, which is what I thought I needed, I would have lost out on a deeper relationship with God and with others. There is a gentleness and loving curiosity that we learn to have for ourselves and others in this journey.

So, give yourself *the gift of time*. We are in the process of healing and this process will draw us closer to God and closer to others. Give yourself genuine tenderness and grace. The process of healing from years of disfunction takes time.

♥ *Dear Jesus, thank you for showing me these things that need to be healed in my family. I present myself, my words, my heart, and my family to you. Please help me to be patient in this process. Inspire me when to speak and when to remain silent. Teach me how to act and when to let go. I can't fix anything, but I trust in your power.*

Tool # 2 - Giving up our Rights

This is, in my opinion, the most powerful tool of all. Much of our pain and so much of the hurt in our world is because we care so much about what other people think.

Consider all the pain, depression, and even suicide associated with social media. On these platforms, people are exposed to a superficial world, one that is deliberately staged, by our friends, family, and idols. Often, dissatisfaction arises when comparing or looking to "greener pastures." Unfortunately, multitudes of individuals get slammed for their posts every day. Sometimes these negative comments devastate people. The words take on power and cause people to feel depressed and angry. Many adolescents are bullied to the point of suicide because of their social media connections.

Have you noticed that posts from certain people cause much hurt and emotional pain, while posts from others, though of the same tone, have no affect at all? Why is this? It has to do with caring. When we care about the relationship, or we feel the other person has power or esteem, their words matter to us. If someone doesn't have a relationship with us, it doesn't affect us the same way.

Giving up our rights is so powerful because it deals with caring about what those closest to us think about us and say to us. Giving up our rights enables us to let go of the expectations for others to love, understand, and accept us perfectly.

Much of dysfunction in unhealthy relationships has to do with trying to earn love and approval from those we care about. Attempting to convey truth, honesty, vulnerability, and authenticity to our loved ones, often results in disapproval, rejection, and conflict. But what if disapproval, rejection, and conflict had no power to hurt us? Could we live a more truthful, honest, vulnerable, and authentic life?

Because this book is faith based, I have tried to continually make connections between our human, earthly dimension, and our spiritual, Christ-centered dimension. So, we look to Jesus and His walk on earth as the model for our relationships. We do have earthly rights, but we don't have greater rights than Jesus did.

Jesus spoke the truth in love. Not everyone approved. So therefore, when we speak the truth in love, not everyone will approve. Jesus said what He believed, thought, and felt, and not everyone accepted it. We can do the same. Jesus was able to love people on earth and not receive love back. He was able to do this because He knew He was already perfectly loved by His father. We can love on earth and not get love back, because we already are loved by our Savior. We can accept others, though they do not accept us, because we are already accepted by God.

Giving up our rights is so powerful because it removes the expectation of others to "get" us in our earthly dimension. It taps into the higher dimension of the perfect love, acceptance, and understanding that God has for us. He is pleased when we live honestly, authentically, and vulnerably. Choosing to live this way will not be understood. It is a higher spiritual walk that models Christ.

There is speaking truth out loud to ourselves in the midst of persecution that allows us to continue to love and forgive. It prevents bitterness and/or thinking of ourselves as a victim. It enables us to speak truthfully because we choose to be honest for the other person's greater good, even though there may be backlash.

- We give up our right to be understood. Christ was not understood.
- We give up our right to be accepted. Christ was not accepted.
- We give up our right to be liked. Christ was not always liked.
- We give up our right to be validated. Christ was not validated.

There are two ways to utilize this. We can say it out loud to ourselves amid mocking, rejection, scoffing, or name calling.

♥ *"Jesus, I give up my right to be understood. You were not understood, so why do think I have that right. I give up the right for _____ to 'get' me. I give up the right to be accepted. You were not accepted by everyone and so I won't be either. I give up my right to be liked, not everyone liked you and not everyone will like me." I give up my right to be validated. You were not always validated, nor will I be.*

The other way to use this is to expect backlash when we make choices for our loved ones highest good. When people don't get their way, or they are called to account, or are confronted about their behavior, they will retaliate. They will twist our words or tell us that we are the problem. When our loved one slams the door, refuses to speak to us, or says they are not hungry and are punishing us by not eating dinner; we hold our ground. Just call out to yourself what it is.

- ♥ *"Oh, so this is the backlash this time." "Thank you for enabling me to give a consequence rather than stuffing my emotions and then raging later."*
- ♥ *"Thank you, God, and I give up my right to be like, loved, understood, accepted and validated. I make the choice to speak honestly with my loved ones. This is for their highest good. Thank you that you have given me the power and grace to be strong."*

Tool # 3 - Talking to God/Prayer

Prayer is conversation with God. It is the pathway of communication between God and man. Just like conversation is the pathway to intimacy with others, prayer is the pathway to intimacy with God. Many people over-spiritualize prayer. Prayer enables us to enter into a sacred connection. I used to believe that prayer required something from me; holiness, reciting particular words or phrases, and even fasting. If I was not actively going to church, it felt hypocritical to pray. It was like, I haven't been practicing my faith with

Church attendance, so God is mad at me...therefore He won't listen to me if I pray.

The truth is we need not do anything to connect with God other than to turn our hearts and attention toward Him in honesty.

Prayer is the weapon we have been given to fight the enemy. Entire books have been written on the subject but let us keep it simple. Prayer is meant to be a continual conversation with God. It can be as uncomplicated as, "I hope I get a good parking place God; you know I am in a rush." Or "God help me to be kind to my kids tonight, you know how tired I am after working all day. I really don't have much to give right now." The major focus for prayer as related to the concepts in this book is comparing truth of scripture to what we are believing. We ask the Holy Spirit to teach us the truth. When we identify beliefs that are lies, we pray and ask God to replace our lies with the truth.

We also ask God which of our actions within our family relationships are based on hurt from our past. Where are we controlling? Where are we unloving or unsafe? Where are we refusing to be honest with our loved ones? We ask God to forgive us and change us. This removes guilt and allows us to connect deeply with God. As we receive greater grace and love in our heart, we are changed in our actions.

Tool # 4 - Saying what is "Most True"

Saying what is "most true" is very powerful. Learning this concept freed me from some of the damage I experienced in spiritually abusive situations. For a while, I attended a church that believed that faith was the key to God healing us from any sickness or disease. There are certainly scriptures that support faith being connected to healing. I would listen to message after message quoting those scriptures but observed a disconnect between the scriptures and what I witnessed in the lives of those who attended the church.

On one occasion, I overheard a parishioner lament his weakness. He felt guilty for taking insulin for the treatment of diabetes he had since childhood. Another time, I had a woman collapse in my arms as she shared with me how weary she was of trying to believe God would heal the late-stage cancer of her husband. Instead of sitting next to him in intensive care the day before he died, she attended a church service. She was trying to muster enough faith to heal him. It was like faith was the power, rather than God being the power. It seemed backwards to me; that the humans were giving the God of the Universe his marching orders, rather than the other way around.

I now think of this type of praying as "faithing it." We Christians know faith is important. The Bible even says that, "Without faith it is impossible to please God," (Hebrews 11:6). Yes, faith is vital. But we cannot fake our faith to God. He already knows our hearts. He knows about our actual circumstances, fears, lack of trust, and weaknesses. How can we be honest in our prayer about our limitations, and still acknowledge, and believe the higher truths of scripture. This is where praying what is "*Most True*" comes in.

Rather than just claiming what God says is true, this process acknowledges the negative emotion that we feel during times of distress. When we say what is MOST TRUE, we first identify the feelings and pain of a particular situation. Then, we state God's truth, which is a higher truth than what we feel. For example, we might pray something like this:

♥ *"God, it is true, that I struggle trusting you and I am a new believer of yours. It is true that the doctors said that I have cancer and that the chemo is not working. It is true that I am afraid, and I am not sure if you will heal me or not. But what is most true is that the Bible says that you died on the cross for all my sin. The Bible states that by your stripes I am healed. It says that you will never stop doing me good. It states that you have good plans for my future. So, Lord God, I ask for you to heal me based on your word, but no matter what, I believe that you are loving me and caring for me in this cancer journey."*

♥ *"God it is true that my daughter is suffering from rejection and the effects of her childhood from being raised in our home. It is true that much of her pain is because of me and my brokenness and unhealed heart since I am her mother. But what is most true is that you are the redeemer of my life and her life. What is most true is that you are the God who works everything for her good. You are the God who makes beauty out of ashes. You are the God who saves to the utmost and you ARE saving my daughter and healing our relationship."*

♥ *"God, it feels upsetting to have made my mother mad when I told her that she can no longer speak to me the way she has in the past. It is true that I feel like I am a bad daughter. But what is most true is that you love me and would never call me names. What is most true is you want me to love myself enough to speak up if I am being hurt in my relationships."*

Tool # 5 - Walking Back Negative Emotions

Negative feelings are indicators, red flags if you will. There is nothing to concern oneself with when our feelings are loving, kind, and positive. Since feelings follow thoughts, negative thoughts are generating negative feelings. Think about this because it is really important. When we feel sad, angry, frustrated, or helpless, it first originated in our mind. Can we feel angry if we have not first had an angry thought? No, it all originates in the mind.

What should we do with negative thoughts? First, our society uses defense mechanisms to rush to feel good when we should actually be feeling our feelings. We use several techniques to avoid dealing with the pain and discomfort of our negative feelings. We use denial, we avoid or "stuff" our legitimate feelings of sadness and anger, or just use our most favorite - distraction, to avoid dealing with pain and discomfort. To be healthy though, sometimes we need to spend time grieving and feeling anger.

When something or someone dies, whether it is a loved one, or the death of a relationship such as divorce; grief and anger are the appropriate emotions. When someone disregards your feelings, screams at you, lies to you, or you are in a lose-lose situation, negative emotions should follow.

Walking back our negative emotions is a process of analyzing and problem solving. It is a problem-solving strategy that is helpful to figure out what triggered the emotion. Once we understand the trigger, we can choose the appropriate actions. There are usually three possible healthy action paths.

1. We can discover that we are believing a lie and therefore make a choice to reframe our negative thoughts.

2. We can discover that the emotion is appropriate for our situation and allow ourselves to feel the feelings that are suitable to our circumstances.

3. We can understand that someone is pushing our boundaries and speak and act accordingly.

This is the process. Once we know why we feel what we are feeling, we can then rationally choose how to respond or act with our family.

- I feel _____ right now. (Negative emotion). Why do I feel _____?
- What have I been thinking about?
- When did this feeling start?
- What occurred right before the feeling?
- What is the belief or thought behind the feeling?

Ponder the answers to the above questions. Then ask:

- Is this related to my family belief system?
- What am I afraid of?
- What are my choices in this situation?
- What is God's highest good?
- Is what I am believing true?

At this point in the problem-solving process, we either say the truth regarding what God says about us, or we allow ourselves to feel the appropriate negative emotion. If we feel overwhelmingly oppressed, we can say the truth statement aloud. The following are examples:

When we fear something terrible will happen:

- If God be for me, who can be against me? Or if God be for "Tina," who can be against her?
- With long life will He satisfy me and show me His salvation.

- For I know the plans God has for me plans not to harm me, but to give me a hope and a future. Or we can substitute our loved one's name.
- God will never stop doing me good.
- No eye has seen, no ear has heard, the things God has prepared for "Tina," because He loves her.

For the nameless feeling of defectiveness and "unlovableness:"

- I am the beautiful one whom God loves.
- I am perfect and God delights in me.
- I am your beloved and you are mine and your banner over me is love.
- You formed me in my mother's womb, and before I was born, you knew me.

For the fear of missing God and that we need to perform to please Him:

- He who began a good work in me will see it through to completion.
- God is the *AUTHOR* and *FINISHER* of my faith.
- It is God at work to *WILL* and to *DO* according to His purpose.
- Even if your heart condemns you, God is greater than your heart.
- He will cause me to walk in His ways.

Often, walking back negative emotions indicate that we are upset because of the words, actions, or neglect of a loved one. When this is the case, we choose if we want to speak or not. If we care about the relationship, we often choose to speak the truth in love. We then may need to apply some of the other tools because this is not always appreciated. We also have the choice of withdrawing or distancing ourselves from the relationship if there are patterns of disrespect.

Tool # 6 - Holding up a Hand

Holding up a hand is a physical technique used to create a boundary between you and another person. Boundary resistant individuals are often unaware of their behavior. Using this technique provides a non-verbal cue to the boundary resistant, that they need to stop or change their behavior.

This is a very effective technique when someone refuses to take your "no," or disrespects what you are saying. It is to be used with words spoken by you in a commanding voice. It places a physical boundary and puts the other person at arms-length. Thus, it emphasizes that you mean what you say, and that the other person is crossing your boundary.

- To use it, stretch out your arm full length and turn your hand at a 90-degree angle so fingers point upward. Fingers will be splayed in the classic "Stop Sign" position.
- Place your hand so that it breaks eye contact with the individual you are confronting.
- Firmly state what the person is doing wrong:
  - "I said, "NO.""
  - "Don't ask me again."
  - "Do not speak to me in that tone."
  - "I am going to leave until you can speak to me without yelling."

Tool # 7 - Assessing Safety and Intimacy

Assessing safety and intimacy is where we use the Traits of Safe People to evaluate how close we should allow other people to get to our hearts. This tool uses the entirety of Chapter 4, *Traits of Safe People* as a tool in and of itself. We get to choose our relationships and who we allow to be close to us. This tool allows us to bypass our "should" and "ought's," and enables us to evaluate our relationships in a detached way.

- The chapter provides insight to assess who you should let close to you and who you should keep at a distance. When we think of boundaries, think about your property. Some people should not be in your yard at all. Some are safe enough to allow onto your front porch. Only a few get to come into your home. Only the absolute safest get to come into the intimacy of your heart/bedroom.

Tool # 8 - Becoming a Cheerleader

People who struggle with codependency believe that they are necessary and that they are wise. This belief cultivates an unintended consequence; our loved ones are not allowed to fully grow to their mature selves. We must resist the inclination to help the overly needy adolescent/adults in our families. Instead, we become their cheerleader. Being a cheerleader means we refrain from helping. We encourage independence from us and dependence on God.

Can we trust that God placed abilities in us to empower us to have a successful life? Can we sit on the sidelines and believe this truth as we cheer our loved ones on? Encouragement now comes in the form of affirmation of the innate wisdom and problem-solving ability God put in each of us. Below are some of the new ways we encourage our loved ones to grow. These are our cheers!

- Bummer, that sounds like a big problem. What are you going to do?
- I know you are so smart. How are you going to handle that?
- That is what I have always loved about you.
- You are smart and figure things out.
- Yikes, that sounds like a God-sized problem. How could He help you?
- What are you thinking is the right thing to do?
- Wow, that is a big one. Have you prayed about it?
- You make good decisions. I know you have what it takes to work through this.
- What am I giving you advise for? You are smart. What are you going to do?
- That is what I have always liked about you. Troubles come, but you and God work them out.
- You have a great brain. What is it telling you?
- What do you think your choices are in this?

Tool # 9 - Detaching

Because of our close connections with our family and especially our children, their suffering and negative emotional circumstances can feel like they are happening to us. Psychologists call this enmeshment. Enmeshment is stronger than empathy. Empathy is understanding, compassion, and being able to put yourself in another person's shoes. Enmeshment is when you stay in those shoes. When we are enmeshed with our loved ones, we feel their emotional angst in a strong way. It's as though the emotions they are feeling are being processed in our bodies and minds.

Detaching is unplugging from the feeling that what is happening to someone else is happening to you. I use my fictional daughter "Tina" as an example.

- We can detach by simply saying aloud, "This is happening to 'Tina.' This is not happening to me."
- Another way to detach, is to ask yourself if you are the main character if this were a story. If not, we again we say aloud, "This is not my lane, nor my problem. I love 'Tina' enough to allow her to *have* her own problems and to *figure out* her own problems. I love her enough to allow her to have her own God story."
- Visualize your loved one as tiny, as a child in God's hand, and you are far away. It is also beneficial to see yourself little. Pray, *"God, I place 'Tina' in your strong capable hands. You say she is your child. I know you are a good father who cares for His children. I allow 'Tina' and myself to be little. I thank you that you are big, strong, and loving."*
- Pray and ask the Holy Spirit to cut any unhealthy emotional or Spiritual ties that might be connecting you to your loved one. Pray, *"Lord, I sever any unhealthy or unholy connections that link me to 'Tina,' in the name of Jesus. I am not her rescuer nor her Savior, you are. I pray that you would strengthen the connection she has to you. Please remove the feeling that what is happening to her is happening to me. I pray that you would use these circumstances for good in her life."*
- Imagine yourself and "Tina" driving in a car. Picture yourself

194

getting out of "Tina's" car and into your own vehicle. Place God in the car with "Tina." Say out loud. *"I thank you, Father, that you are with 'Tina' on this journey. Please help me stay in my own lane."*

- Visualize yourself little and then jump onto God's lap. Then picture "Tina" as little as well, sitting on God's other knee. It is extremely comforting to embrace the reality of our littleness and it helps with detachment. My absolute favorite Bible verse of all time is the following because weakness and littleness are power.

My grace is sufficient for My power is made perfect in weakness.
—2 Corinthians 12:9 NIV

Tool # 10 – Surrender: Silent on the Outside, Praying on the Inside

Surrender is difficult because it is a supreme act of faith. It is extremely powerful because it is counterintuitive. It goes against our natural inclination which is to control our circumstances. It doesn't seem natural to not take action and leave a situation solely in God's hands. Normally, we depend on ourselves to solve personal problems and to control the outcomes of those we love.

Surrendering control is especially difficult because we are often correct when we discern the harm and potential destructive paths of our loved ones. We want to control, but hopefully understand now, that doing so violates another's free will. That is why surrendering is so powerful, because we discern the pitfalls ahead as we resist rushing in to fix everything. Trusting God by surrendering, feels as though we are doing nothing in the face of dire circumstances.

The kind of surrendering I am speaking about, is not "doing nothing." This new way of surrendering is a "silent on the outside, faith and trust on the inside practice." We aim to be at peace and may be silent as far as words spoken aloud, but we are activating God's power. We are not actually silent inside. We are praying. Rather than thinking-fixing, thinking-fixing, thinking-fixing; we are praying-releasing, praying-releasing, praying-releasing.

Self-awareness is needed, as we resist directing and controlling. Rather, we send glancing prayers upward. These momentary prayers to God are part of what the Bible calls abiding. He is *WITH* us. All it takes is a moment of directing our thoughts and hearts toward Him for us to become aware of His guidance and power. We enter a silent and abiding dialogue…

♥ *"God? Speak or be silent?" "Intervene or let go?" … You WILL hear. You WILL have an urging or checking feeling, that will direct you. Instead of "US" telling others what they should and ought to do, we ask God to show them.*

♥ *Little prayers like, "Thank you God for directing them." Please turn their hearts toward you God. I know you love them and want a relationship with them. Help them in this Lord." And then let go… This is the power of surrender.*

Try out this powerful practice and watch God move on your loved one's behalf. You will not be disappointed.

Tool # 11 – Reframing

The Bible talks about taking every thought captive. The teachings of God indicate that we are not helpless against negative thoughts. Though this concept has been taught in scripture for over 2,000 years, its power has been extolled by psychologist only in the last few decades.

> *We demolish arguments and every pretension that sets itself up against the knowledge of God, and we take captive every thought to make it obedient to Christ.*
> —Corinthians 10:5

What we think about matters. Depression, anxiety, and suicidal thoughts are increased during negative thinking. The current term used by psychologist for the process of replacing a negative thought with a positive one is "reframing." The Bible calls it renewing your mind.

We are instructed to think about what we are thinking about. We are to evaluate our thoughts, and if our thoughts, "Exalt themselves above the knowledge of God," we are instructed to take action. This action is choosing to think a different thought. We replace the negative thought with a positive one.

There is glorious positivity in the Bible. We never have a problem that we have to handle alone. We no longer have just our own power, but we now have God's power active and available in every circumstance.

When we are in a spiral of negativity, thinking worse case scenarios, we are allowing our thoughts to exalt themselves above the knowledge of God. This means we are imagining our circumstances as though we are Saviorless. *(Read Tool # 5 - Walking Back Negative Emotions to help in this process.)*

You will discover that the negative emotions come from "stinky thinking," a lie the dark one has allowed you to embrace. Now that you know what's broken, fix it! Allow God's truth about you and your intentions to be revealed. Intentionally place the Savior's positivity about you and your actions forefront in your mind. Reaffirm your relationship with God or simply thank Him for revealing the lie.

- Sample Thought - *My boss might be angry at me because I told him I could not take over all my co-worker's responsibilities during her maternity leave.* Reframe: *I am so proud of myself that I was able to speak up and get the help I need to cover for my coworker during her maternity leave. I have choices and I am loving myself by speaking up.*
- Sample Thought - *Oh no! My husband is upset that I refused to listen to him when he wouldn't stop shouting at me.* Reframe. *It is awesome that I am teaching my husband how to speak to me. I know he has the ability to control himself because I am the only person he speaks to in this way. This is backlash. It is uncomfortable, but this is good.*
- Sample Thought - *"Here we go again. Nothing ever goes my way."* Reframe: *"It is God at work in me to will and to act according to His good pleasure. (Philippians 2:13) So I thank you God that you will work out this situation for my good."*

Tool # 12 - Making Friends with Yourself; a Process

This tool is designed to help you begin loving and receiving yourself in a deeper way. Its use will enable you to love yourself more and to share yourself in all your beauty and strengths, as well as weaknesses with those you deem worthy of you.

Many of us know ourselves well enough to describe ourselves as having "parts." There may be a public self or persona you put on, and then a private reserved self. There may be a creative leader within you and a reluctant hider who is afraid to take the lead. There may be a part of you that wants to fit the worldly ideal of physical beauty and a part of you that just wants to be loved for who and how they are. It is time to make friends with every part of yourself.

This tool is an ongoing process. Whenever we realize that we feel inwardly conflicted, like we have two selves, we can make friends with both those sides of us. Both sides constitute the "real us." We may have allowed, or chosen one side to dominate because of fear, or lack of self-confidence. This process embraces, and recognizes that we are lovely, complex individuals.

- While in prayer or meditation, introduce your two sides to one another.
- *"Chris who isolates, meet, Chris the star of the show. Ordinary Chris, meet extraordinary Chris! Imagine them meeting, hugging, and loving one another.*
- You may see the two sides merge into one "you."
- Imagine your heart opening like a flower enfolding as it blossoms. Allow both sides to feel the deep love and compassion you have for yourself.

Tool # 13 - Inner Healing Prayer

Inner healing prayer is when you ask the Holy Spirit to show you "WHY?" you feel, believe, react, or function in a particular way. It is a very deep and powerful tool used in Christian counseling. It is used to get to the root of the "Why?" behind behavior and beliefs. The "Whys?" behind our, behavior, feelings, words, reactions, and beliefs are sometimes based upon the big life events of our past.

Inner Healing Prayer is a technique in which we ask the Holy Spirit to show us the root of our lies.

Inner Healing Prayer is a powerful and specific healing technique that I learned from my friend and mentor, Tammy Melton. If what you are about to read resonates with you, I suggest you purchase her book, or take one of her *Inner Healing Prayer* workshops at: https://www.legacyministries.info/inner-healing-prayer.html

This technique is useful when there is a specific unrest, uncomfortable feeling, or a particular negative emotion, like anger, depression, sadness, or feelings of inadequacy. Basically, it is useful in any circumstance of emotional or spiritual struggle, especially when they reoccur. These patterns of struggle are described in the New Testament as strongholds, areas of pain and sin because a dark force has been given an open doorway to oppress an individual.

Many times, when dealing with these strongholds, we have made heart vows or promises of how we will function, care for, or protect ourselves to avoid future pain. These personal vows are lies, as they are independent of God's promise for us. The goal of this healing is to ask our *TRUE LORD JESUS* to show us where or how we came to believe a particular lie. I was taught to ask "True Lord Jesus" to speak, because the Bible says that Satan can disguise himself as an angel of light or take beautiful forms. Thus, I call upon the one and only True Lord Jesus during this healing. This is probably a bit legalistic and asking God or the Holy Spirit is fine. But I, personally use the phrase, "True Lord Jesus."

True Lord Jesus will give someone asking, an image, memory, or impression of something from our past. Once we have the memory or impression, we ask Him to show us how we came to form the belief, or any lies we came to believe when this painful event happened. We ask Him if there were any vows or promises we made in our heart at the time. *YOU WILL* have a memory come and an understanding as to what you came to believe as a result of the event.

Please do not be afraid because this is often a very emotional moment. It is normal to cry because there is an underground pain that has been stuffed and is coming up for healing.

Please, please do not be afraid to allow God to show up and heal you. God is the gentlest of Fathers. When He heals us, He places His fingertip on one tiny thing at a time. He will never, never, blast you with pain that you cannot cope with. He will also never embarrass you or cause you shame. If you are not in a safe place, He may withhold Himself until you are better positioned to receive.

Typically, people pray at the end of a discussion, or after having a dialogue with someone who is troubled in some way. During normal times, our prayers go something like this. A friend tells you something they are struggling with or distressed about. We discuss it for a while and then at the end of our discussion, we figure out a solution and pray for it to occur.

We might pray, "God please remove this depression." Or "God, please take away the nightmares that 'Tina' has been having." Or "God, please help 'Tina' to let go of her anger towards _____."

We ask God to heal, give, teach, or reveal something that would meet the need of the troubled individual.

When using Inner Healing Prayer, we ask God *why* someone is struggling in this exact moment. We directly ask God to show, teach, or demonstrate *why* the person is experiencing a problem in the first place. Inner healing prayer is basically asking the Holy Spirit to guide healing and go to the root of the issue.

We ask Jesus to show the person who is struggling "*why?*" they are feeling so depressed. "*Why?*" they are having nightmares. "*Why?*" they want to avoid close relationships with people, "*why?*" they feel shame, "*why?*" they feel they have to still stay connected to someone who is continually verbally abusive.

Inner Healing Prayer is usually a two-person process. It is tremendously important to ask God to guide one's questions and time together before beginning. One person is the facilitator; "the pray-er," question asker, and recorder. The other is the person in need.

Person "A" asks questions led by the Holy Spirit and takes notes. Person "B" listens to the questions and then meditates silently, listening to the Holy Spirit for the "*WHY?*" to be revealed. Here are some sample questions:

1. "Where did this feeling come from?"

2. "What is the root of this memory?"

3. "Why does _____ feel this way?"

4. How did "Tina" come to believe _____?"

The recorder takes quick short-hand notes documenting the words of the person seeking God. There may be words that come to their mind, or a memory, a song, or an impression which comes to them as they wait in silence. This process can be done alone, but in that case, no one will take notes. It is just silent prayer asking the Holy Spirit "Why?"

Below is a sample of a healing that God provided for me when I was alone using. I had no recorder…

> Me: *"True Lord Jesus, why do I feel so disconnected from the Holy Spirit? I feel close to you Father, I feel close to you Jesus, but why do I not feel as close to the Holy Spirit?"*
> Jesus: (Image of being yelled at by my dad.)
> Me: *"True Lord Jesus what does this image of being yelled at by my dad mean?"*
> Jesus: *"You think of the Holy Spirit as the disciplinarian, the one who corrects and points out all of your mistakes. Since you were never disciplined in gentleness by your earthly father, you assume that the Holy Spirit is harsh."*
> Me: *"Holy Spirit, I am sorry for rejecting you. I want to be close to you as you really are. I break agreement with the lie that says that you are a harsh disciplinarian. True Lord Jesus, what is the truth in place of this lie."*
> Jesus: *"The Holy Spirit is the force of all good and all love in this earth. Anything that is good is from God. Therefore, the Holy Spirit will only guide you to good things, things that are good for you."*
> Me: *"In place of the lie that the Holy Spirit is harsh, I speak the truth. The Holy Spirit is the force of all good in my life. His directions are gentle and for my good. He would with-hold no good thing from me. As He guides and directs me, it will be in directions that are for my benefit.*

Thank you, God! What do you want to fill me with in place of the lie I just released to you?"

Jesus: *"I give you power, intimacy and closeness with the Holy Spirit."*

Me: *"Thank you Father. I receive power, intimacy, and closeness with the Holy Spirit in place of the pain of the harsh discipline of my past. Thank you."*

Facilitator's Tips

THANK YOU FOR STEPPING up to facilitate a small group. Thank you for allowing God to use the gift of leadership He placed within you to help others. This curriculum is a guide and you most likely will not fully discuss every single thing in each chapter. Trust yourself and trust God in you. Prepare to be amazed by God.

The chapters in this book are designed to provide information, personal insight, and connection with one's heart. The lessons can be completed alone, in a family setting, with a partner or in a small group. It is my belief that the small group setting is ideal because deepest learning occurs in collaboration with others. Our learning is multiplied because the perceptions of our fellow group members activate deeper connections within us.

When organizing a small group study, your job as facilitator is vital. The facilitator is not the teacher, per se. The Holy Spirit is the teacher. The facilitator will direct the flow of the lesson, lead the group discussion questions and transitions to the next activity. The facilitator calls on others to speak. Like all good teachers, the facilitator adds insight and connection between what others are saying, what is being taught in the chapter, and what they are thinking of themselves.

When organizing the class, a two-hour block once per week is ideal. "Chunk" your time into forty-minute segments. The first forty is for review and discussion of the reading for the week. The next forty is for the discussion questions, while the last forty are for art, discussion of the art, and prayer.

In my experience, the Holy Spirit will move and teach most deeply during the art, discussion, and prayer portion, so it is best to protect that time of the class.

Like all teachers, you have a plan, and you are prepared, but how everything flows and how your "students" learn is out of your hands. You, as the facilitator, will set up the room before everyone arrives. Have the art supplies arranged for easy sharing. Know the chapter and the questions, and then go with the flow. The ideal room set up has some tables, hook up for a computer or TV and perhaps a white board. (My first class was in my basement so no worries if you do not have the ideal set up!)

The goal of facilitating is to create a safe environment with regard to transparency and vulnerability. This means that you will be the one to set the tone. You may need to go first and share. Share how your week went, and not just the pretty parts. If you have a past of dysfunction, it will be helpful to others if you can tell a bit about yourself and why you chose to facilitate this group. What has God done for you? How has He changed you? What is He doing now in your life?

When the group begins to trust one another and share the not so pretty parts of their past that God is healing, please tell them, "Thank you for trusting this group with the sacred pains of your heart. We are worthy of your trust. It is an honor that you would share with us." Sometimes people may cry. Place your arm around them and tell them that what happened in unhealthy family systems deserve to be cried over. God cried too. They deserve to be loved and cherished.

Each week before you begin, have a quick "check-in" with the members of the group. If you have too many women attending to be able to listen to individually, you can "pair and share." Have them turn to the person next to them and share one high and one low of the past week. Every person may not be able to connect with you, but you can facilitate their connection with one another.

If you have more than six women in your group, you will need to organize them into smaller groups. You can have a whole group discussion on the reading of the chapter for the first forty minutes. Then break them into smaller groups for the art, discussion of the art, and prayer portion of the lesson. It is a good idea to ask the members who feel comfortable praying aloud for the other members of the group, to lead their group. Prayer at the end is vital and we don 't necessarily want all the introverts in one group. Place "the pray-ers" strategically in the small groups as mini-facilitators. Encourage them to read this portion of the book.

You may want to consider having a closed group after week two of class. We want to develop deep safe relationships and having new members come in and out may hinder this. Begin a signup sheet with the contact information for a future group.

Some of the group members will arrive late every single week. Some members may have a commitment that requires them to come a few minutes late. Our lives are busy, and we cannot arrive on time for every single thing. But… START ON TIME! END ON TIME! It is not fair to those who are punctual to delay the class, or to end up missing some of the class if they need to depart at the scheduled time.

As you teach, you will notice, that times and flow need to be adjusted. Feel free to adjust. All teachers do this based on the needs of the group. You might consider taking a group consensus or vote about how the class is run. This promotes ownership and connectedness.

When the art portion of the class begins, there will be questions. We are trained to want to do things "right." There is no "right way" in this class. Often the Holy Spirit will give something that is not what was "instructed." Tell the group to draw, write or compose whatever they feel led to create. It will be awesome!

Often, someone will have a "blank." This is especially prevalent if there was a large amount of dysfunction. Not remembering much is a way God protects us. In fact, I asked God to show me the minimum I needed to recall to be whole. Please do not encourage digging into the past. The Holy Spirit will bring up little things in a gentle manner.

When someone draws a blank, tell them that is normal and to draw what they can. You can point them in a different direction. They could create a word splash, poem, an acrostic poem, or a song. Sometimes a scripture or song might come to their mind. Have them write that out in colorful markers. The Holy Spirit is out of the box and the art will be too!

Below are common questions that arise and the answers to possible questions.

1. My parents were divorced, and I had different families at various times. *Draw whatever one is coming to your mind.*

2. We moved around a lot, so I had many homes. *Choose one that the Holy Spirit puts on your mind.*

3. I can't remember much, and I am "drawing a blank." *That is quite common, especially if there was a lot of dysfunction. Draw what you can and don't try to force it.*

4. No picture is coming to me. *Write words or create a word-splash, or poem. Maybe a scripture or song is coming to your mind. Write down the words instead of a picture.*

- A word splash is when a person makes a list of words connected to a particular subject.
- Poems can be free verse or rhyming.
- An Acrostic poem is easy to do as well. See below.

  C - caring
  H - hard at times
  O - opens doorways of our heart
  I - individualized
  C - creates freedom
  E - emancipates us

5. Some of the group members will feel led to continue or create art during the week outside of the group. Celebrate this and allow them to share their creations at the beginning or end of the class.

Much of this book is directed by the Holy Spirit. But the Bible says that we see in part and we prophesy in part. Discussion is *GOOD!* I do not expect every person to agree with everything in this book. Though I have prayed and done my best to not misrepresent God, I know some of what I have written may be controversial. The main thing is to teach the concept of respectful, and loving communication…especially if someone disagrees.

On page 211 I have listed the Class Guidelines. It is vital that every single week these are read out loud. They establish the sanctity and the safety of the group.

So…if I could set these four things in stone each week, these are the vital aspects of the class.

1. Pray out loud with the group before class check-in. Welcome the Holy Spirit. Ask Him to protect the class time together. Ask Him to make each individual a trustworthy, safe person. Ask the Holy Spirit to protect us from the temptation to gossip. Pray to prepare hearts and ask God to bring to mind anything He wants to reveal and heal. Ask Him to give each participant the strength and courage to be real and transparent.

2. Before the art begins, give full directions about how to do the art. Make sure your groups are already divided. Then pray for the group out loud. After that, have the women pray silently and sit in silence until an image is formed in their minds. Then they may quietly begin the art portion when they feel led to do so. The art is done in silence. You do the art too. You can share first and model vulnerability and transparency.

3. Before you dismiss, pray a cleansing prayer over the group. Release any pain, or heaviness to God. Remind Him that He carried all our sin, shame, and pain on the cross, so we release everything to Him. We ask Him to cleanse us from carrying the pain of our classmate's stories.

4. Read out loud the following Class Guidelines each week.

Class Guidelines

- Start on Time. End on Time
- The expected outcome is not "Great Art."
- By creating: We allow parts of our brain access to our hearts and this brings greater pathways to receive God.
- The most important part of all of this is *YOU*. Are you trustworthy? It is a tremendous betrayal for us to tell someone else's story to a friend or family member.
- Watch yourself for codependency. Call each other out on codependent behaviors. Our love for one another wants to fix.
- Telling others what they "have to" or "need to" do is not recommended. We encourage by sharing our testimony and pointing to Jesus, telling the way He helped us in a similar situation. We respect others' points of view, especially those who are not followers of Christ.
- Be sensitive to the amount of time each person talks. Some of us are extroverts and may inadvertently monopolize the conversations of the group. If you are a "talker" you are a great gift. You often are the one who is willing to be vulnerable first, willing to share, and this makes others feel safe. We pay special attention when an introvert trusts enough to share.
- Graphic or detailed depictions of abuse is not allowed.
- Each person may "pass" if they do not want to talk, no questions asked.

Glossary

Acting Inappropriately to Get Another Person to Behave Appropriately –Using an unsafe behavior such as screaming, hitting, or cursing to manipulate or control a person who is doing something wrong, e.g., spanking a child to get them to stop hitting, or cursing at someone because you feel disrespected.

Appeasing – The act of tiptoeing around a person or walking on eggshells. Allowing a difficult person to behave inappropriately or abusively to avoid conflict or backlash.

Authentic - Conforms to one's true self and therefore worthy of trust, reliance, or belief. I.e., trustworthy or genuine.

Authoritarian - A parenting style whereby one has dominant power and influence to control or make decisions. In my use, a strict, by-the-law, disciplinarian with little flexibility or negotiations between the adult and child.

Belief Grid – An invisible and subconscious system of evaluating and receiving truth. Acts as a filter in which truth is disregarded if it contradicts beliefs learned in childhood.

Boundaries – Visible as well as invisible lines of separation that divide an individual and what belongs to him from that which belongs to another. These lines can be physical, emotional, psychological, and spiritual.

Choicelessness – Living as though you have no power to choose or change your circumstances. Choicelessness is a result of an abusive family system.

Codependent - Relating to a relationship in which one person is overly dependent in an unhealthy way on someone who has addiction or self-destructive behaviors.

Detaching - Unplugging from the feeling that what is happening to someone else is happening to you.

Don't Talk Rule – Using manipulative, confrontational, or distracting tactics to avoid conversation about legitimate problems, flaws, and behaviors. e.g., yelling "shut up" at someone who is trying to talk; bringing up someone else's flaws and sins when being confronted with your own; or saying that you don't want to talk about something whenever someone wants to have a discussion.

Dysfunctional - A relationship that is flawed and doesn't operate correctly, caused by someone that deviates from normal and accepted social behavior.

Extended Family - Family members beyond traditional Parent/Child relationship, i.e., Grandparents, Aunt, Uncle, Cousin etc.

Family System – A group of people who live together and function as one emotional unit. Complex connections are formed, and unspoken roles are assigned to each family member.

Fantasy Relationships – Holding onto an ideal of what is hoped for or expected in another person. Individuals choose the "fantasy" even when confronted with evidence that the person being fantasized about is not fitting or fulfilling the ideal.

Forgiveness - A conscious decision to let go of past grudges or lingering anger against a person, regardless of whether they actually deserve your forgiveness.

Gaslighting – Being told that one's perception of reality is incorrect or wrong, even though their perception is correct. Often used to cover for a dysfunctional or abusive person.

God's Glory, Our Glory – The concept that each person is worthy, loved, and meant to connect with others in a particular way that no one else can fulfill. Since individuals are created by God, each person's unique gifts, talents, and day to day life is meant to glorify God. We most fully glorify God when we live as His children and are true to ourselves.

Guilt – A feeling of conviction or remorse after doing something morally wrong or unjust.

Highest Good - The best long-term benefit for our family member. This can be physical, spiritual or financial.

Junior Holy Spirit – A form of spiritual abuse when a person considers themselves the spokesperson for God and uses God and His word to continually correct and try to control the behavior of another person. A form of judgement.

Love - Speaking, behaving and acting on behalf of another for their highest good.

Opportunity Cost – The cost or consequence that is incurred when one makes a choice.

Owning Your Power – Recognizing and accepting that in every situation one has choice.

Permissive - A parenting style that is tolerant of something, often something of which others would disapprove.

Problem is Not the Problem; Talking about the Problem is the Problem – A technique used to turn the tables on a person who is bringing up a legitimate issue. Shifting the responsibility, blame, or focus from a problem in a direction that puts another person on the defensive.

Reframing - To redescribe or rethink something from a different perspective; to relabel. Usually refers changing a negative into a positive. It is the modern term for renewing your mind.

Safe - Free from risk, danger, harm, or damage.

Salvation - Deliverance from the power or penalty of sin; redemption. Believed by Christians to be brought about by faith in Christ.

Shame – A negative emotion, similar to guilt but stronger. A belief that one is defective in one's created being, unworthy of love or connection.

Spiritual Abuse - Misuse of religion to control, correct, or gaslight another person for selfish means, i.e., Using God's name to control another's behavior, or to justify one's misbehavior.

Stuffing – Denying and refusing to handle negative emotions in a timely and appropriate manner to the point of inner pressure and emotional buildup. Often results in an emotional explosion in disproportion to an actual event. Is used often with appeasing difficult family members.

Vulnerability – Open to risk, danger, rejection, and judgement. Choosing to be true to oneself and allow others to see one's weaknesses and not just strengths. Necessary for true intimacy to develop. A choice.

YOU Matter!

Dear Reader,

This page is for your personal journey. Please take the time to record your hopes and dreams for your family relationships. Faithful is our God.

HEALING MY FAMILY:

- Describe your family as it is now. Imagine what healing in relationships would look like in your family. Describe that. Dream big.

_____

_____

_____

_____

_____

_____

AREAS FOR IMPROVEMENT/BREAKTHROUGH:

- If _____happened, I would consider it a God empowered breakthrough in my relationships.
- List all family members and a specific hope for healing in relationships.

_____
_____
_____
_____
_____
_____
_____
_____

PRAYER STRATEGIES:

- List prayers of praying what is "Most True."

_____
_____
_____

- What are you thanking God for even though it has not yet occurred?

_____
_____
_____

- Have you ever sung songs to God or praised Him even though your circumstances were dire? This is called giving the "Sacrifice of Praise." It is a powerful prayer strategy. Describe when you did this and the effects on your prayers.

_____
_____
_____
_____

ANSWERED PRAYER:

_____

_____

_____

_____

_____

_____

MYSELF:

I recognized that I cannot change nor save anyone. Instead, I choose to believe that God will help me to change and that my changing will help heal my family relationships.

- If _____

  _____changes in me, I will feel _____

  _____

- What would that look like? _____

  _____

- How would that affect your heart? _____

  _____

- Would it feel uncomfortable, scary, risky, good?

_____

_____

PRAYER POINTS:

_____

_____

_____

_____

_____

SCRIPTURES, IMAGES DURING PRAYER, MEANINGFUL SONGS, OR WORDS FROM THE HOLY SPIRIT:

_____

_____

_____

_____

_____

_____

_____

ANSWERED PRAYERS:

_____

_____

_____

_____

_____

_____

MY FAMILY MEMBERS:

If _____happens, I will feel or achieve

_____

_____

- What would that look like?

_____

_____

_____

- How could that affect the family dynamics?

_____

_____

_____

PRAYER POINTS:

_____

_____

_____

_____

_____

SCRIPTURES, IMAGES DURING PRAYER, MEANINGFUL SONGS, OR WORDS FROM THE HOLY SPIRIT:

_____

_____

_____

_____

_____

_____

ANSWERED PRAYER:

_____

_____

_____

_____

_____

_____

_____

MY FAMILY UNIT:

If _____happens in the

way we relate to one another, I will feel _____

_____

_____

_____

- Describe what that will look like:

_____

_____

_____

_____

_____

PRAYER POINTS:

_____

_____

_____

_____

_____

SCRIPTURES, IMAGES DURING PRAYER, MEANINGFUL SONGS, OR WORDS FROM THE HOLY SPIRIT:

_____

_____

_____

_____

_____

ANSWERED PRAYERS:

_____

_____

_____

_____

_____

_____

How are you different after reading this book?

_____

_____

_____

_____

_____

What do you believe is possible?

_____

_____

_____

_____

_____

With the power of God's grace, is there a focus or commitment that you have made toward the way YOU function in family relationships? Describe that:

_____

_____

_____

_____

Made in the USA
Columbia, SC
31 July 2021

42630653R00130